MANAGING PROJECT INTEGRATION

The books in the Project Management Essential Library series provide project managers with new skills and innovative approaches to the fundamentals of effectively managing projects.

Additional titles in the series include:

Managing Projects for Value, John C. Goodpasture

Effective Work Breakdown Structures, Gregory T. Haugan

Project Planning and Scheduling, Gregory T. Haugan

Managing Project Quality, Timothy J. Kloppenborg and Joseph A. Petrick

Project Measurement, Steve Neuendorf

Project Estimating and Cost Management, Parviz F. Rad

Project Risk Management: A Proactive Approach, Paul S. Royer

MANAGEMENTCONCEPTS

www.managementconcepts.com

MANAGING PROJECT INTEGRATION

Denis F. Cioffi

⫝ MANAGEMENTCONCEPTS

Vienna, Virginia

MANAGEMENTCONCEPTS

8230 Leesburg Pike, Suite 800
Vienna, VA 22182
(703) 790-9595
Fax: (703) 790-1371
www.managementconcepts.com

Printed in the United States of America

Library of Congress Cataloging-in-Publication Data
Cioffi, Denis Felix.
  Managing project integration/Denis F. Cioffi.
      p. cm.—(Project management essential library)
  Includes bibliographical references and index.
  ISBN 1-56726-134-5 (pbk.)
    1. Project management. I. Title. II. Series.

  HD69.P75 C498 2002
  658.4′04—dc21

                                                        2002071868

About the Author

Denis F. Cioffi, Ph.D., a professor in the Department of Management Science, is Director of the Project Management Program, School of Business and Public Management, at The George Washington University.

Dr. Cioffi received a B.S. from the State University of New York at Albany, an M.A. from the University of Virginia, and a Ph.D. in astrophysics from the University of Colorado. After several years of astrophysics research (at the University of California at Berkeley, NASA Goddard Space Flight Center, and North Carolina State University), he made a transition to management by becoming an Associate Program Director at the National Science Foundation. Dr. Cioffi spent 1996 in the Executive Office of the President, where he was a Senior Policy Analyst in the Office of Science and Technology Policy. He returned to academia with a position at George Mason University, where he was a Research Fellow at the Center for Science, Trade, and Technology Policy.

Table of Contents

Preface

Death Star II

Darth Vader walks down the ramp in the main docking bay of the new Death Star to greet its project manager, err, commander, Moff JerJerrod.

JERJERROD: Lord Vader, this is an unexpected pleasure. We're honored by your presence.

VADER: You may dispense with the pleasantries, Commander. I'm here to put you back on schedule.

(The commander turns ashen and begins to shake.)

JERJERROD: I assure you, Lord Vader, my men are working as fast as they can.

VADER: Perhaps I can find new ways to motivate them.

JERJERROD: I tell you, this station will be operational as planned.

VADER: The Emperor does not share your optimistic appraisal of the situation.

JERJERROD: But he asks the impossible. I need more men.

VADER: Then perhaps you can tell him when he arrives.

JERJERROD: (aghast) The Emperor's coming here?

VADER: That is correct, Commander. And he is most displeased with your apparent lack of progress.

JERJERROD: We shall double our efforts.

VADER: I hope so, Commander, for your sake. The Emperor is not as forgiving as I am.

What's wrong with this scene from George Lucas's *Star Wars, Episode VI, Return of the Jedi*? Schedule is discussed without regard to scope or cost: there's no integration!

This book, part of the Project Management Essential Library series, takes a broad, mostly high-level perspective in examining integration in project management. As part of the series, it touches briefly on important and sometimes closely related subjects such as scope management, change control, budgeting, and estimating. A couple of particular topics within these related subjects are, however, treated in detail.

The level of the book assumes prior knowledge of project management. (Two recommended basic project management books are *Project Management: A Managerial Approach*, by Meredith and Mantel, and *The Fast Forward MBA in Project Management*, by Verzuh; see the Bibliography for details.) For example, the reader should be familiar with the usual project management terminology, which often serves as a start to a more complete understanding of fundamental integration concepts.

Because project managers must exercise judgment both in using tools and in working with people, this book deals with management spirit (e.g., sharing information, integrity) as well as mechanics (e.g., work breakdown structure, earned-value analysis). The reader's acquaintance with some basic project management calculations and tools helps in advancing to a more integrated use of these tools in an expanded, inclusive approach.

That said, none of the topics demands such rigor that a beginner could not come away with a good appreciation of the important issues in managing projects. By supplementing the text with a basic introduction to project management, even a neophyte can understand integration concepts, at least on an intellectual level.

For any project manager, more difficult than the intellectual understanding may be coming to terms personally with the comprehensive management approach that true integration calls for. Given equal competence in using the right tools, the more successful project manager will be the one who understands the spirit of integration and thus enjoys and benefits from good working relationships with all who have an interest in the project.

This book will point new project managers and team members in the right direction. More experienced project managers can sharpen their skills, view and handle projects more systematically, and understand better why well-integrated projects meet the triple constraint of budget, schedule, and scope while also meeting customer expectations and ensuring satisfaction.

Denis F. Cioffi

CHAPTER 1

Introduction to the Calculus of Integration

B y definition, integrators seek to include. Although written mostly within the context of a single project, this book takes a broad view of integration, beyond the limited notion of a coherent approach only to a project's triple constraint of budget, schedule, and scope. The historical foundation of mathematical integration turns out to have relevance to modern knowledge management and hence, modern project management. Thus, we begin by examining the meaning of the term integration and discover that a co-inventor of calculus was 300 years ahead of his time in thinking about knowledge management.

HISTORICAL OVERVIEW

At least several papers in the literature (e.g., see Bibliography notes 4, 5, and 28), as noted in Meredith and Mantel [21] discuss particular templates for the traditional coordination of budget, schedule, and scope. And while project management texts recognize the importance of integration, most give a only few pages to its explicit mention. In his discussion of the growth of project management from its "traditional" ways, Kerzner [18] writes that "modern" project management demands integration skills of its practitioners, and he quotes several specialists who testify to the critical importance of these skills. Kerzner also reminds us that the global project manager faces especially difficult integration problems.

The Project Management Book of Knowledge (PMBOK®) [25] advocates the standard approach to "project integration management," dealing with plan development, execution, and change. In contrast, this book views integration as expressed in 1967 in a classic paper in the *Harvard Business Review* [19] as "the achievement of unity of effort."

The authors of "New Management Job: The Integrator" did not use the words "project management," which they may not have recognized as a discipline in 1967, but they indicated the primary area that the integrator should handle: "the nonroutine." They also anticipated "rapid rates" of change that would drive organizations to operate "like R&D-intensive firms"—in other words, companies would work with projects, and projects need integrators.

More than 30 years later, in a special series by the Industrial Research Institute dedicated to *Succeeding in Technological Innovation*, another author discussed management of the "innovation process" and wrote that it requires "a dedicated full-time coordinator-integrator," who should communicate well and be skillful both technically and in business. [22]

Whatever the description and whatever the locale, effective integration management in projects comprises two inherent components: hard work and a good attitude (which itself often requires hard work). Good project plans are not static until after the project ends. Project changes mandate continuous iteration and integration of project plans. As Frame observed, reluctantly but realistically, "between 50 and 65 percent of our project budgets is dedicated to chasing paper." [13] Much of this paperwork, now with a huge electronic component, is rightfully driven by the integration concerns of managing the project and its plans and personnel.

A SPECIFIC YET GENERAL CONCEPT

Analogous to the worries of a project manager watching the real-time changes of any project variable affecting the triple constraint, the branch of mathematics called calculus deals with (among other things) varying rates of change. In project management, one deals with costs, schedules, and scope, which can change frequently, sometimes erratically. Change is a fact of project life.

In calculus, to integrate means to sum, and one approximates reality with more accuracy by summing finer and finer elements. In project management, only by bringing together cost, schedule, and scope elements in sufficient detail can one produce a true picture of a project.

Project managers should view their projects as systems. Leibniz, a cofounder (with Newton) of calculus, conceived of integration mathematics broadly. In fact, Leibniz is credited with the conception of a formal system. [6]

Leibniz described the integral technically as "the sum of all lines," but more generally he saw his creation as a structure "for the acquisition and organization of knowledge." [9] And that's what project integration is all about: Data, information, and knowledge related to all aspects of a project are acquired, organized, and assembled to present a coherent picture of the project's status. In today's parlance, these efforts are called knowledge management. In a project environment, one must also manage the people who can provide or transmit relevant information. Thus, project integration management harnesses the tool of knowledge management to pursue unity of effort.

PROJECT MANAGEMENT AS INTEGRATION MANAGEMENT

The words "integrate" and "integration" have meanings outside the sphere of mathematics. To integrate means to "make entire or complete," and integration represents creating the whole "by adding together or combining separate parts." [8]

If only some fraction of a project's separate parts is being managed, a project is not being managed in an integrated manner. An individual may feel responsible for a budget or a schedule or a scope—but who integrates and begins managing the project? Even if the fraction approaches 100 percent, the project is not necessarily being managed systematically (i.e., as a system). If not integrated, the project is, by definition, only partially managed. To say, therefore, that one is managing a project implies integration management.

The expanded notion taken in this book sets an even higher standard. If a project manager integrates budget, schedule, and scope, but is not concerned with the so-called stakeholders and the people on the project team, the integration task is incomplete.

The following chapters describe particular areas within the management of a project where integration is especially important, or where a certain tool or process furthers integration efforts. Chapter 2 examines the concept of knowledge more thoroughly and begins the discussion of integration management with the idea of sharing information from the start. Much of integration occurs in the development of the project plan, and thus the major section of this book, Chapter 3, is devoted to this topic. Chapter 4 takes a new look at earned-value analysis, which is a major integration tool.

In the context of integration, Chapter 5 looks briefly at people issues, and Chapter 6 discusses integrity. In many ways, the most difficult and important discussion takes place in Chapter 6. If all the project's processes and special techniques are planned and prepared correctly, but there is no integrity, the project will fail.

CHAPTER 2

Integration through Shared Information

Project integration begins with sharing information to combine the budget, schedule, and scope consistently. This chapter treats briefly the differences between data, information, and knowledge, and it suggests at what organizational levels each should be shared. Three paths to project integration are noted, and a possible explanation of the big difficulty in integrating large projects is offered. Finally, some guidelines for presenting information are placed in the context of managing projects.

DATA, INFORMATION, AND KNOWLEDGE

With only a slight narrowing of meaning [8], one can say that "data" are the numbers taken directly from measurements. In the hierarchy of knowledge, data provide the firmament, the fundamental basis of all higher applications, and ultimately, one hopes, of decisions.

Data are the basic facts that will be used to begin to understand the project. Valuable data collection begins with an eye toward the triple constraint: cost data, schedule data, and scope data. In managing the project, especially in the execution stage, the project manager requires organized data that reflect the health of the project. These data will facilitate the integration of budget, schedule, and scope. Instead of a single schedule number (e.g., "the project is three weeks ahead of schedule"), the project manager asks for many numbers presented coherently.

The data must therefore be somehow processed, or manipulated. They are organized, given a context. When sufficiently organized, they are considered factual. They have become information because by virtue of their organization they have "informed," i.e., they have been transported from an isolated existence to reside in some structure where they communicate; they tell a story.

From its beginning in the late 20th century, information technology has enabled rapid communication and analysis of information. Information technology holds the potential to transform 21st-century life, including project management. Quick access to relevant project information should improve the integration of projects. For all but the smallest projects, the project manager should be able to depend on assistants to collect data and begin their transformation into the "information" the project manager needs.

"Knowledge" sits another level up on the hierarchy that has data at its base. Similar to the manner in which data are transformed into information, information can be transformed into knowledge. This transformation process is, however, more formal. Information is codified, and so its context is determined with more structure than the corresponding data transformation (to information). With this formality, knowledge is seen as the intellectual perception of information. [8] Knowledge of a project may also include a subjective judgment based on objective information.

Managing projects in an integrated manner means managing information. But will this recognition and deeper understanding change behavior? Placing project management number-crunching in this framework implies that project managers and their hierarchical superiors should provide conditions that encourage, at a minimum, sharing data to improve project integration. Even better conditions encourage communications that turn shared data into information. Information should be shared within and across projects and programs.

With much additional effort, the shared information can be filtered, sharpened, archived, and made accessible to all in the organization. In other words, the information should be transformed into knowledge. From the perspective of knowledge management, effecting this transformation is the major objective of an organization's project management office. Business strategists see knowledge as the basis upon which modern organizations grow and prosper. Establishing this process takes resources, and maintaining the culture requires a commitment from senior management.

Furthermore, the commitment can be expanded to communicate new knowledge to the project management profession as a whole. The Project Management Institute has recognized this responsibility for its members (e.g., in its *Role Delineation Study*, 24). Professions advance as their practitioners replace standard practices with best practices. This large-scale professional maturation can occur only if the best practices are distilled and communicated.

New knowledge does not help current or future projects succeed until the knowledge is utilized. Utilization begins with understanding, which sometimes requires bringing together heretofore disparate pieces of knowledge. This ability to create understanding through synthesis resides in people, and a good project manager wants people on the project team who can acquire, understand, organize, and utilize knowledge—or, in Leibniz's terms, who can integrate.

Disparate pieces of knowledge can best be understood and integrated by a team with multiple perspectives (discussed in Chapter 5). This very diversity can make integration difficult at the start, but with perseverance team members will see different areas in which this new, integrated knowledge can be applied. A team with secure members will share the knowledge, expanding the number of personnel aware of it. Workers will then be able to use this knowledge to solve problems in projects that further the organization's goals. In the course of solving problems, new data, information, and knowledge will be gained, and the cycle can continue (see Figure 2-1, Knowledge Management Cycle for Integration Management).

Managing and motivating this process does not occur in a vacuum. Acquisition of data and information—and the subsequent transformation of information into knowledge—require resources. An organization with a commitment to solving problems and managing projects well allows its personnel time to acquire and understand information. It also give them the tools to do so, and where necessary, provides training. The cycle might be summarized as: generate (data); transform (into information); transform again (into knowledge); document; archive; make accessible; communicate; train. Although not mandatory, often a project management office is used for the latter four functions, as depicted in Figure 2-1.

But when the speed of modern business is sometimes described with the phrase "Internet time" to reflect its quickness, can a project team always afford to wait for knowledge? In the short term, insight is even better than the standard production and utilization of knowledge: Insight permits a quantum jump from data to utilization without dawdling at information and perhaps skipping even knowledge. This jump is often termed "innovation," and it cannot easily exist without the ready availability of shared data.

INTEGRATION WITHIN A PROJECT, A PROGRAM, A COMPANY

Integration in the context of projects is usually taken to mean integration of the cost, schedule, and scope of an individual project. This book expands that notion to consider integration more holistically as a bringing together of data, information, knowledge, and people to meet a project's triple constraint. The context of project integration can be widened further to consider a project's roles within the parent organization.

FIGURE 2-1 Knowledge Management Cycle for Integration Management

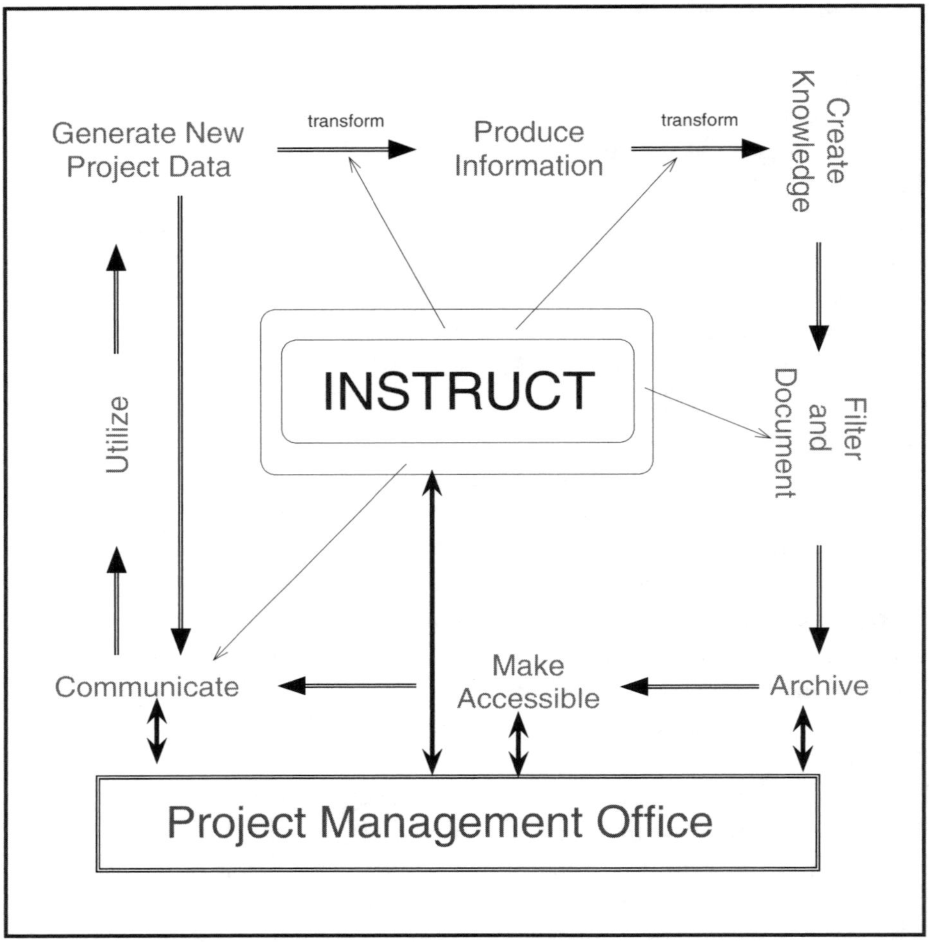

Generate New Project Data — transform → Produce Information — transform → Create Knowledge

Utilize

INSTRUCT

Filter and Document

Communicate ← Make Accessible ← Archive

Project Management Office

Within the individual project, mostly data and information are shared and integrated. But consider the advantage of sharing the distilled knowledge from many projects across programs, throughout the organization, to ensure that all projects fit the organization's strategic objectives—in other words, to ensure that the company's goals and projects are integrated. The hierarchy presented in Figure 2-2 shows how projects can be positioned so that they further the organization's vision.

An organization should share knowledge at its highest levels. Its senior executives should translate the organization's vision and mission into strategies that produce a consistent portfolio of programs.

FIGURE 2-2	Positioning Projects to Further the Organization's Vision

Organizational Vision
Organizational Mission
Organizational Strategy
        Portfolio of Programs
        Portfolios of Projects within Programs

Tactics to Effect Strategies
        A Pipeline of Projects
        Integrated Management of Multiple Projects
        Integrated Management of Individual Projects
        Process and Task Management

Senior executives and program managers then create a spectrum of projects within each program. The choice of the initial projects creates a pipeline of projects. With modern enterprise software systems, these projects can be integrated collectively and individually.

What are some of the disadvantages of not taking such a systematic approach? To begin with, projects become driven by people instead of policies or themes, and project support shifts when individuals move on. Projects may or may not have anything to do with the organization's objectives, as seen (on any given day) by senior management. The project pipeline becomes chaotic, and programs mostly battle over turf. In short, the organization begins to look like many organizations: dysfunctional. In this environment, integrated project management is not likely to thrive.

In contrast, what are some of the advantages of a systematic approach? First, the organization moves in a coordinated way, even if in a variety of directions. Next, accidental duplication of large-scale effort is avoided. Perhaps even more important, program managers and project managers can assist each other when working on similar projects or tasks. Data, information, and knowledge become accessible to all, preventing wheel reinventions. Across program areas, shared project information and global knowledge lead to consistency of the organization's projects' plans for cost, schedule, and scope.

This notion of consistency and sharing within an organization can and should be extended to the project management profession and the larger communities within which project managers work. Common goals on a large scale require significant effort at up-front communication and cooperation. Initially, the process will generate frustration as people with different perspectives and somewhat different goals try to talk with each other, but the final results will show the rewards.

THREE POSSIBLE PATHS TO INTEGRATION

An organization can take three possible paths to integration. The discordant path is the least efficient and, from the vantage point of the maturity of an organization's project management culture, the most immature. Little communication and accidental agreements characterize this route to an integrated project. Plans for budget, schedule, and scope proceed almost independently until circumstances force interactions. At the end of a project, success is defined by meeting (or coming close to meeting) only one axis of the triple constraint.

The second way, which is probably the most common, might be called the consilient path. Consilience means a "jumping together" to arrive at a common understanding by taking different routes. [8] In the consilient integration process, various parts of the system work semi-independently, with some cooperation, because they have the same general end goals. Because of this overall agreement on the project, high-level integration occurs eventually, but detailed, real-time integrations can lag.

For example, in one large governmental organization, before a division could release a request for proposals, it had to be approved by about a dozen people at headquarters. Internal procedures required obtaining the first few signatures serially, but the remaining ones could proceed in parallel. Included in that second set were the organization's lawyers. When the employee who was responsible for obtaining the signatures once suggested going to the lawyers simultaneously with the others, his hierarchical superiors instructed him to put the lawyers last, because, he was told, they tend to cause trouble.

But the lawyers were part of the team, weren't they? And they couldn't be bypassed, could they? So why not get them on board from the beginning, when their knowledge and expertise could assist (or even cause discord) sooner rather than later, and then adjustments could be made sooner rather than later? In this particular instance, a lawyer spotted a subtle omission in a document and prevented a potentially embarrassing international situation.

So consilient paths to integration can work, but instead why not agree to cooperate fully and to integrate the project from the start? Organizations with the most mature project management cultures integrate from the very beginning, which is the best way to integrate both projects and programs. The organizational infrastructure and its processes ease and promote the sharing of knowledge, and the compensation system rewards cooperative activities. Good project managers will prefer this last path to integration, which despite the possibility of early pain (e.g., more time with the lawyers), promises a better project at the end.

WHAT MAKES A PROJECT LARGE?

Communicating information, so necessary for project integration, becomes more difficult as a project grows in size. But how does one measure the size of a project? In cost? Schedule? Scope? Typically the budget scales linearly with the number of tasks and the number of people, so why does it seem that managing a large-budget (or large-schedule or large-scope) project is more difficult, proportionally, than managing a small-budget project? Although the budget, schedule, and scope all are obviously important indicators of the size of a project, the efficient transmission, receipt, and comprehension of data and information may be the single most relevant criterion, for only then can the project be integrated. Does the linear scaling of cost with tasks break down? Consider the following.

A system with n_c nodes of communication has a number, N_{ch}, of communication channels between the nodes, where

$$N_{ch} = \frac{n_c(n_c - 1)}{2} \propto n_c^2. \tag{2.1}$$

The proportionality to n_c^2, which becomes more accurate as n_c becomes much greater than 1, means that the number of channels grows as the square of the number of nodes, i.e., n_{ch} grows geometrically, not linearly (see Figure 2-3). To zeroth order, in any project where communication between workers is essential, whether so-called knowledge workers (e.g., software development) or not (e.g., cement pourers), the number of communication nodes equals the number of workers. (If outside systems are involved, the number of nodes can be higher than the number of internal workers.)

The total number of messages sent, N_m, is the product of the number of nodes and the average number of messages per node, n_m, viz $N_m = n_c n_m$. But most likely, because individuals respond to incoming messages as well as generate new messages, the number of messages per node is directly proportional to the number of nodes: $n_m \propto n_c$. As one might have expected initially (by arguing simply that the total number of messages is directly proportional to the total number of channels), the total number of messages is therefore also proportional to the square of the number of nodes:

FIGURE 2–3   The Number of Communication Channels Grows As the Square of the Number of Nodes

Numbers below each diagram show n_nodes (N_channels).

Rightmost column shows additional channels over the sum of the first two groups (equals the square of the number of nodes in each group)

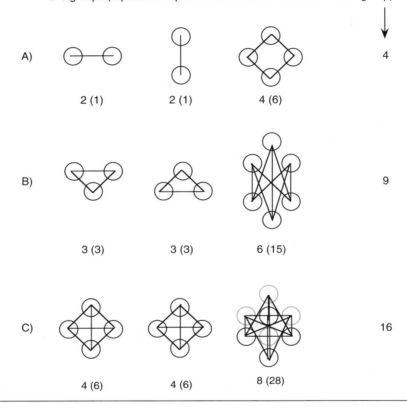

A)

2 (1)   2 (1)   4 (6)   4

B)

3 (3)   3 (3)   6 (15)   9

C)

4 (6)   4 (6)   8 (28)   16

$$N_m \propto n_c^2. \tag{2.2}$$

In the limit that each individual receives information or data at a rate that they can be understood fully and integrated with other relevant project information, an increasing number of messages represents an increase in understanding. The more messages one receives, each containing valid data, the more one understands the integrated progress of the project. However, in addition to having information associated with these messages, the messages come with an associated cost (if nothing else, the time to read them). If the number of messages per node increases beyond some limiting number, n_m^*, efficiency decreases and the project's integration suffers.

Bureaucracies grow as intermediaries are installed to keep the average number of messages for decision-makers of order n_m^*, such that $n_m^{dm} \lesssim n_m^* < n_m$, where n_m^{dm} is the average number of messages per decision-making node. The new intermediate nodes represent a local increase in the number of nodes, in the hope of maintaining a local limit ($\lesssim n_m^*$) on the number of messages at the decision-making nodes (with each message containing better than average information, one hopes). The global number of messages, however, continues to grow as the square of the total number of nodes, n_c, which has increased.

Since the total information content (which must initially contain redundancies and misleading or even false information) of the project management system is roughly proportional to the total number of messages, N_m, the total information, I, is also growing as the square of the number of nodes:

$$I \propto n_c^2. \tag{2.3}$$

At this point, the nodes might better be termed information nodes.

These suppositions may explain that a large amount of information makes a project large. The information that must be handled grows as the square of the number of nodes, but budgets usually grow linearly, at best. That is, if making 1 widget costs \$1 in personnel costs, \$100 is budgeted to make 100. (Imagined economies of scale are often used to justify cutting budgets below the linear extrapolation.) But larger projects may be inherently more difficult because linear resource increases do not keep pace with the geometrically growing information content, and integrating the project becomes more and more difficult. How much more difficult?

Let us speculate further. Surely the effort needed to integrate information initially grows nonlinearly with the amount of information that must be integrated. Because connections must be made among all the information quanta (whatever they are), it seems not unreasonable to argue that the first integration efforts go as, say, the square of the quanta, i.e., of the individual packets of information. If, remembering Leibniz, we represent the integration effort with a solitary integral sign, $\int$ (you may use any symbol you like), that relationship would be written $\int \propto I^2$: The effort to integrate information is proportional to the square of the total amount of information. Because we have no real knowledge about this exponent, other than to argue that it is greater than 1 (but does learning allow it to fall below 1 as the project proceeds?), the relationship can be written more generally:

$$\int \propto I^y, \tag{2.4}$$

where y may change as a function of time.

Combining this general relationship with the proportionality between information and the number of nodes yields:

$$\int \propto n_c^{2y}.$$ (2.5)

Even if the integration effort were only linear ($y = 1$), we would still be left with the proportionality to the square of the number of nodes. If the exponent y is only 5/3—and above we postulated that it might be closer to 2—doubling the number of communication nodes increases the integration effort by a factor of 10! From the perspective of integrating information communicated over many channels, then, perhaps large projects are difficult to manage precisely because they contain so much information, and resources are rarely scaled accordingly. Studies of successful projects may be able to verify this conjecture.

PRESENTING INFORMATION

How is the objective of sharing integrated information accomplished? At least two components are involved: (1) the physical infrastructure needed for distributing, collating, archiving, and searching for electronic information, and (2) the skills needed for effective presentation of information.

For large projects, the first component demands the services of hardware and software experts in information systems and technology. The right system can certainly facilitate achieving data integration goals. However, no system can overcome the absence of the right attitude toward integration. This attitude (and the resources to accompany it!) must permeate the organization, starting with the people at the top of the organization. The story is told, for example, that when Lou Gerstner became head of IBM, he asked what fraction of its (full-time-equivalent) personnel were involved in current projects. The answer he received, eventually, was about 140 percent, making real integration impossible. Under Gerstner's leadership, the percentage was brought down to a more reasonable level (around 80 percent).

The presentation of information, on the other hand, has been studied for thousands of years. In the computer age, despite (or because of) the ease of producing and displaying data and quantitative information, the clarity, information content, and effectiveness of the average chart has probably deteriorated.

Especially in this digital age (we have no technological excuses now), words, numbers, text, and images should be integrated to tell a story and answer questions about a project, especially one in progress. Edward R. Tufte has written three excellent books [29, 30, 31] that explore the presentation of information in detail. For example, he aptly describes one major communication challenge of project management: How can one best present evidence about a project to assist colleagues and hierarchical superiors in making decisions? The question can be framed more realistically as: How can one best present project information to prod colleagues and hierarchical superiors to make or support decisions that point the project in the direction desired by the presenter?

The presenter should have a point of view that is grounded in the project data. Good managers make decisions based on strong arguments and valid information, and clever presentations are legitimately useful tools. Rather than being perceived cynically in terms of an attempt to manipulate both the data and the receivers of data, a good, honest presentation displays truthful evidence in the manner that best suggests the desired direction; in fact, the desired direction is the direction suggested by the proper interpretation of the information! The creation of such a display should be inspired by the need to help colleagues understand important facts in the shortest possible time.

Some of Tufte's other advice applies to communicating integrated project data and information (e.g., earned-value data). [32] For example:

1. *Enforce visual comparisons.* The human eye-brain system can compare spatially adjacent data much more easily than temporally adjacent data. Present project data not in a vacuum but in comparison to other data, from the same or similar projects, within the same eyespan.
2. *Show causality, and show it quantitatively.* Again, project data are not to be presented for the sake of displaying numbers. The information presented should at least attempt to explain some aspect of the project's progress. In the numerically driven management system that is project management, quantities should accompany the causality mechanism proffered.
3. *Show multivariate data.* Projects are complex, and the data needed to explain them fully are complex. Humans can understand information at great density; explain, don't dumb down.
4. *Present high-quality content with integrity.* The display should reveal the truth. Presenting information well takes work. In general, do not be satisfied with the first graph or table produced by your favorite software. For that matter, do not let the software dictate the data presented or the format of the presentation. After data have been integrated, a huge part of managing a project is communicating relevant information so that it too can be integrated. Choose and present well, and you will ease the task of project integration.

CHAPTER 3

Project Plan Development

The first major integration of the project's budget, schedule, and scope occurs in the development stage of the project, when the project team creates its detailed plan. At a minimum, that plan contains the project's work breakdown structure, a budget, a linear responsibility matrix, a network diagram, and a schedule. This chapter explains how the project team combines historical information and the cost rates found in the parent organization's resource breakdown structure to make tradeoffs between resource use and schedule time to build an integrated project plan. A full understanding of these tradeoffs depends on the concept of a task's optimum duration.

PRE-PROJECT: THE RESOURCE BREAKDOWN STRUCTURE

Ideally, at the conception of every project, the project manager will have the opportunity to examine a structured presentation of the organization's resources (or, more likely, some subset that is relevant to a family of project types). Analogous to the work breakdown structure (WBS), a resource breakdown structure (RBS) puts the possible resources and their cost rates into a hierarchical tree. This tree can then be used at the lowest levels of a project's WBS to determine the cost of the project.

In the steady state of the organization, the creation of the RBS should pre-date any project, and thus it should not be the responsibility of the project manager. Details on the utility of this explicit integration of scope and cost can be found in Chapter 3 of *Project Estimating and Cost Management*, one of the books in this series. [26]

The discussion of resources requires quick agreement on terminology. First, do not consider money a resource in the pre-project stage. Instead, anything that requires funding, whether directly or indirectly, is a resource—and resources cost money. For example, renting a particular piece of equipment, whether a bulldozer or a computer, costs so much per day. Obtaining a free permit costs money because a worker's effort is required, and the worker will be compensated. If the permit itself has an associated cost, the cost of that resource is correspondingly increased. Also important is cost rate information about each resource, that is, the cost per unit time or, if the unit is to be purchased, the cost per unit.

A brief aside on dimensions is warranted. Effort is the product of a specific quantity of a particular resource, i.e., its intensity (e.g., two programmers), and the duration through which it is used. The most common example uses a solitary worker for a day, which yields a worker-day of effort. When multiplied by the cost rate obtained from the RBS, the effort is transformed into cost. In this single calculation, we see the integration of scope (with resources), schedule (through the duration of the effort with that resource), and budget (through the cost rate).

If one knows beforehand the exact effort required to accomplish a given task, the duration of the task will be given by the effort divided by the resources used. If the duration of a task is fixed and the effort is known, the amount of full-time-equivalent workers is given by the effort divided by the duration. Thus, if one calculates effort, the correct end result will have the dimensions of a resource times time, whatever the unit (e.g., bricklayer–weeks, bulldozer–days, programmer–hours, lawyer–minutes). So despite the oft-seen statements about projects having a total "effort" measured in so many accumulated hours, these individual task efforts—proverbial apples and oranges—cannot be added to each other unless the units are identical.

When managing projects:

1) [**Effort**] equals [**Resource Intensity**] times [**Task Duration**]
2) [**Cost**] equals [**Effort**] times [**Cost Rate**]

Thus, only efforts with the same units may be added to each other.

In any given project, the relatively small fraction of totally new tasks deserves the concentrated attention of the project team. Together with valid historical cost data, a good RBS makes it easier for a manager to direct attention to the tasks that require it. Thus, the lack of a good RBS puts a project manager at a disadvantage. Although the manager is always ultimately responsible for overseeing cost estimates, ideally the time is spent contemplating only the more challenging estimates.

INITIAL FOCUS ON INTEGRATING RESOURCES, COSTS, AND SCHEDULE

A project should not be deemed successful until it achieves its final deliverable. A project can, however, start to fail long before that deliverable's end date. The project manager and the project team should set the foundation of success at the start. Planning takes much time and energy; moreover, it costs money. Too often the attitude is, "We don't have time to do it right, but we have time to do it over." As Edison is reputed to have said, "There's a better way."

Integration Begins at Project Conception

Once the project begins, how does one describe its progression? Projects have lives, and in those lives they go through phases. The phases overlap. For our purposes, a project's life is divided into four phases: conception, development, execution or implementation, and closeout.

Integration begins at project conception by establishing the attitude that all formally involved with the project will concern themselves with integration (define as "unity of effort"). Whether by design or by accident, the person at the top of any organizational division sets the tone for the personnel in the branches below that stage of the hierarchy. The person at the top of the project in the conception stage may not be the project manager—who may not yet have been chosen—but instead may be the project sponsor or the project champion, typically people at a higher level in the organizational hierarchy. Their responsibility to set the right integration tone is correspondingly higher.

These initial integration efforts will include not only integration of resources, costs, and schedule, but also integration of people. The "people" category comprises project management experts, technical experts, and any parties at interest, i.e., those who will be affected by the project (often called stakeholders, an overused and now insufficiently descriptive term because it implies consideration of only those having an immediate and direct stake in the project).

The project manager has established the right attitude among the team members if the project team embraces the idea of the "greater team" [3]; see Figure 3-1. The greater team comprises any population outside the immediate project team that the project may affect, whether directly or indirectly.

Members of the greater team may include the project sponsor or its chief advocate within the organization (its champion), other project teams in the

FIGURE 3–1　　The Greater Team

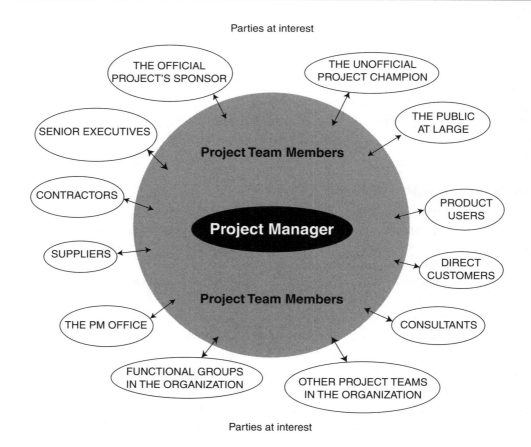

organization, the project management office, suppliers, consultants, contractors, functional groups in the organization, the public, and not only the client but also the client's customers. Ferreting out the indirect effects of the project requires considering the project's long-term as well as immediate implications. Paradoxically, because they are not so intimately involved, individuals of the greater team farthest away from some imaginative center of team effort, where the project team lies, may be the first to understand the more indirect or subtle consequences of a project.

The project manager must of course exercise judgment in determining the greater team. Too often project teams fail to ascertain the specific needs of customers. (For example, because of political infighting, designers of the

Denver International Airport were forced to work initially without formal interactions with the principal users, Continental and United Airlines. [17]). Before the project team can finalize detailed planning, the concerns of all parties at interest must be discussed thoughtfully and honestly, and those concerns should carry some weight in the integration of cost, schedule, and scope. Once aware of all consequences (technical and political), the project team may occasionally decide that a given concern should carry no weight; henceforth it will be ignored.

A Communications Plan As a Key Integration Tool

Not only the project itself, but also communications about the project must be managed. In general, communication is the essence of project management. In particular, communication of valid information lies at the heart of project integration.

Thus, at this early stage of project planning, after the project team has determined the parties at interest, the next step in furthering project integration is to develop a comprehensive communications plan. This plan should describe the use of the physical communications infrastructure as well as prescribe and possibly create the organizational interconnections that will facilitate delivery of relevant information, in the proper time frame, to the appropriate members of the project team and the greater team.

Modern communication methods, especially the Internet and intranets, make a comprehensive system increasingly feasible. Boston's "Big Dig" is an example of a project run amok: years behind schedule, billions of dollars over budget, and in the past, important information often hidden. But for all its troubles, there is now one shining part of the Big Dig project: its external communications system. A recent visit to www.bigdig.com provided current traffic advisories related to Big Dig activities, a copy of a letter from the Massachusetts Alliance for Small Contractors concerning proposed revisions in transportation rules, and even an article from *The Washington Post* that is critical of the project's management.

Valuable message content should claim the highest priority, but one should not overlook the importance of message frequency. Both project workers and managers will likely give low priority to or even ignore too-frequent communications. In the minds of many who receive such communications, the high frequency tends to reduce the significance of the messages, irrespective of their actual content. The ease of delivering a quick e-mail to one or many people somehow causes many senders to forget the time involved in—and hence the cost of—opening, reading, and responding to that e-mail.

Therefore, a communications plan should guide when, where, how, and who as well as what and why.

With the proper integration spirit, "what" will include references to schedule, cost, and scope. Similarly, planners will predetermine "when" to communicate not merely by the calendar, but also by the project schedule and budget. For example, the team can plan explicitly to communicate via meetings or e-mail when the project has spent a certain fraction of its budget, reached a similar fraction of its planned total duration, and simultaneously completed the appropriate parts of its scope. (The discussion of earned value in Chapter 4 illustrates one technique for formally integrating this information.) Thus, the communications plan fulfills its role as a key integration tool in two ways: (1) it brings the greater team together in assessing the progress of the project, and (2) done properly, the messages force project managers to consider a project's progress in an integrated way.

Deliverable Milestones

At this point in project planning, the project manager has assembled a diverse team, and team members have embraced an integrative attitude as a result of the approach of senior executives and the project manager. The team has determined the parties at interest and created a communications plan. What might the team communicate first? After communicating its existence and its willingness to listen to members of the greater team, the project team should explain the largest-scale deliverables and their approximate costs and scheduled dates of delivery—in other words, present an integrated milestone picture.

Technically, milestones themselves have no duration; they serve as markers of significant events. The beginnings and endings of tasks are usually considered significant events within a project. Completion of the largest parts of a project represents the most significant events. For our purposes here, any distinction between the completion (i.e., the end) of a deliverable and the deliverable itself is being ignored; these milestones typically have a one-to-one correspondence with the first-level elements of the work breakdown structure. At this top level of the WBS, no disagreement with the deliverables mandate should be even considered, much less permitted. This level of the WBS contains the major components of the project (e.g., the big subsystems in a computer program, the large physical objects and supporting infrastructure in a construction project) and, if the client wants to examine them, the project management plans (an often-forgotten component and associated cost).

The selection of these top-level deliverables marks the first real definition of the project beyond the initial scope discussions. By virtue of their deliverable nature, these top-level elements help make more concrete the large-scale scope of the project. Senior executives and experienced project managers can estimate gross top-down costs (equivalent to those derived from the summed efforts) without the details that can come later from a bottom-up estimate in conjunction with the resource breakdown structure.

Continuing the process, again in consultation with project managers and based on prior experience, senior executives suggest the approximate total durations of the high-level elements (which come from the efforts through the resource intensity). With the durations, one can begin to think about a schedule.

A detailed schedule is not possible now, but perhaps even more important is a network diagram that shows the causal relationships (if there are any) among the milestone deliverables. This milestone network diagram can be used to create the first, rough schedule, and the project is off to a good, integrated start.

The uniqueness of each project means that all involved should understand the approximate nature of these initial cost and time estimates. Senior project managers often complain about how quickly their hierarchical superiors can forget, when convenient, all the caveats and "abouts" that accompany these first, rough numbers, which attempt an initial description of a project in terms of the triple constraint. Stories abound of projects (and their managers) being held to unrealistic demands because of wishful, undisciplined, and unintegrated thinking by those who should know better.

A Deliverable WBS Anchors Integration

A good project manager will consider the project as a system and use all necessary tools in conjunction to present a consistent, comprehensive picture of the project both as planned and in progress. The work breakdown structure anchors the planning. If communication lies at the subjective heart of project management integration, the WBS lies at its objective center.

Project managers and workers, being human, will respond subjectively to all but the simplest messages. These subjective responses mandate an external fixed standard upon which the team can agree, and that standard is a deliverable WBS. It must communicate simple, unambiguous messages.

The better the WBS, the more deliverable its orientation—ultimately to the exclusion of all activities (i.e., verbs) as well as the modifier "oriented."

The more deliverable the WBS, the more it will further project integration—and help prevent scope creep.

If one writes, "subroutine Z" or "widget A" in the WBS instead of "design widget A," or "design subroutine Z," the team comes to understand the reality of this specific widget or subroutine, which is unlike the other widgets and subroutines in the project. Similarly, instead of "subsystem approval," the deliverable WBS says, "Vice President's signature, for subsystem approval." Thus, a better term than "deliverable-oriented" defines this high standard: "unambiguously deliverable." The concept is so important that it deserves its own initials: DWBS. The deliverable work breakdown structure should always be used in place of an unadorned WBS (whatever its orientation).

The members of the team may not all agree on whether the design for a widget or a subroutine has been completed successfully, but they should be able to agree on whether the widget or subroutine exists. ("What does it mean?" asked the Dean of the business school when reporting to the faculty about the progress of the new building, "when we are told that the design is 60 percent complete? Have they only designed three of the five floors, or are all the floors there, but not the walls and doors?") Presumably one would not need to be so precise as to distinguish between the existence of functioning vs. shell widgets or subroutines. If the object does not function fully (i.e., according to scope specifications), it does not fulfill its role in the DWBS or, more important, in the reality of the project.

The DWBS for the project contains the specific details of the project that make it a project—i.e., something new and something finite in scope as well as time. A generic WBS can deliver only an outline for projects of similar type, but the DWBS for the project can be the DWBS for only that project; it is a tautology.

One light example of a minimalist DWBS may begin to show the power of this technique. For an evening gathering of the board of directors of a local community organization, the hosting family was asked to provide coffee and a room for the members to congregate. The request qualified as a minor project. It had a smaller scope than other projects of that type (e.g., parties) that the hosts had produced many times previously, and it seemed to contain the same elements. The DWBS, if it had been created, might have looked as depicted in Figure 3-2.

This structure was not created, of course, and the hosts, who themselves normally drank caffeinated coffee, kept only a few beans of decaf in the house for the occasional cup, but not nearly enough for the 15 to 20 people

FIGURE 3–2   DWBS for a Local Board Meeting

Project Name: Coffee

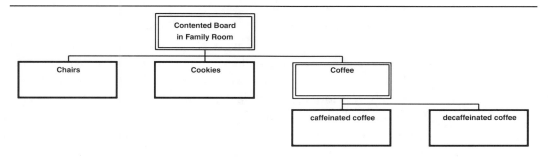

expected—all of whom, as it turned out, wanted decaffeinated coffee that night. Unfortunately, most readers will know of more serious omissions in projects either planned or executed, such as buildings without bathrooms, newly paved roads without telephone poles reinstalled (true story), or a computer operating system with a button labeled "start" but with no "off" button. From the beginning, therefore, because people see the specifics of what is being produced, a deliverable work breakdown structure encourages good design.

The generally positive attributes of the DWBS are further amplified when they are considered with respect to integration. First, from the perspective of the client for whom the team works, implicit in the word "deliverable" is an event at which some object is in fact delivered, and an event occurs at some point in time: a schedule.

Second, the DWBS has made the project's scope real and explicit. The total cost of the project will itself be broken down and associated clearly with every element of the work breakdown structure; an intelligent client prefers to pay for results, not activities. From the client's perspective, integration of budget with schedule and scope begins directly with the construction of a deliverable work breakdown structure. However, before seeing how the DWBS can drive a detailed budget, the concept of the optimum duration must be understood.

The Minimum Effort and the Optimum Duration

In the planning stage of a project, the manager with an integration mindset will not differentiate priorities among the three components of the triple constraint. However, the scope of a project does not lend itself to an informative graphical presentation. Whether through wishful thinking or good project discipline, one often considers the scope fixed while continuing to entertain variations in schedule and budget.

A proper understanding of the relationship between schedule and cost requires appreciating fully the concept of the optimum duration of a task, which can then be generalized to the optimum duration of the project. A fast-paced economy often mandates that some projects will need to deliver products within the shortest reasonable duration, not the optimum one, thereby allowing immediate project costs to rise in the hope of maximizing revenue on some larger timescale. Nonetheless, the optimum-duration concept remains important.

Effort—the product of resource intensity and duration—is not necessarily fixed for a given task. That is, the effort (e.g., the worker-hours) needed to accomplish the task depends on the resources used in a way that is not linearly proportional to the resource intensity. (For example, many simple tasks around the home require less than half the time when the resource intensity is doubled from one person to two; the required effort therefore has shrunk.) Thus, the effort equation is properly written:

$$E_R(\alpha) = R_I \Delta t(\alpha) \qquad\qquad 3.1$$

where E_R is the effort produced with resource R, and the subscript reminds us that efforts resulting from the use of different resources cannot be combined meaningfully. R_I is the resource's intensity (i.e., how much of it was used), $\Delta t(\alpha)$ is the duration through which the resource works, and the parameter α models the duration's dependence on the resources; the exact α dependence is unimportant for now. The optimum duration, Δt^*, is the duration at which the effort required is a minimum, E_R^*, and thus the cost (through the RBS resource rate) is too, i.e., at $\Delta t = \Delta t^*$, $E_R = E_R^*$ and $R_I = R_I^*$, where E_R^* is the minimum effort needed to accomplish a specific task using resource R at intensity R_I^*. At the optimum duration, the resource use is also termed optimum for that particular task.

In the linear approximation that humans seem to find intuitive, a doubling of the duration of the time allowed for a task implies a halving of the resources needed for that task. Given a specific task already accomplished, with specific resources used throughout a given period of time, the product produced by multiplying those resources by the duration equals the effort.

Will that number equal the effort required for the same task executed within a different duration or with a different resource intensity? Only in the linear approximation can one assume constant effort for a given task, independent of the resources needed; i.e., in the linear approximation, E_R is constant, and $\Delta t(\alpha) \to \Delta t = E_R \div R_I$, independent of R_I.

Although often implicitly assumed, in real life the linear approximation holds only in a narrow range about the optimum use of resources. Therefore, when integrating the schedule with the budget, one cannot necessarily compensate for a decreased duration with resources increased proportionally.

To understand better how to approach such a situation, the parameters can be portrayed graphically by considering a task with a known minimum effort and optimum resource intensity, E_R^* and R_I^*, respectively. Normalize all quantities to their optimum values by defining $E \equiv E_R / E_R^*$ and $R \equiv R_I / R_I^*$. The minimum effort ($E=1$) and the optimum resource intensity ($R=1$) determine the optimum duration, where $\Delta t = \Delta t^*$.

Figure 3-3 presents a schematic example of how the effort required for a task may increase as one moves away from the optimum resource use. For representational purposes only, the graph was produced by building the α dependence directly into the effort, viz $E \propto R^\alpha$, with $-1 < \alpha < 1$; $\alpha = 0$ in the linear approximation. Brooks's famous line that adding programmers to a late software project will only make it later [7] would correspond to $\alpha > 1$, i.e., both the duration and the effort increase when resources are added. But in the hope that better management would move the project out of that regimen, the graph in Figure 3-3 uses $\alpha = 0.5$. Since $\Delta t \propto R_I^{\alpha-1}$, the duration of a task increases when fewer resources are provided ($R < 1$), and it decreases with more resources ($R > 1$).

Remember that a decrease in duration does not imply improved or even sustained efficiency. One must compare the change in duration to the change expected in the linear case of constant effort. Similarly, an increased duration may or may not correspond to diminished efficiency, i.e., although taking more time than originally planned, the task could require less time than it would have taken if the effort had stayed constant. What is the point? Because the change in duration alone does not provide the necessary information, project managers should instead consider a task's effort as a function of resource intensity.

As the resource intensity changes, the effort may decrease ($E < 1$), increase ($E > 1$), or remain constant ($E = 1$). Given sufficient historical data, an organization could show the true relationship between resource intensity and effort

FIGURE 3–3   Optimum Duration

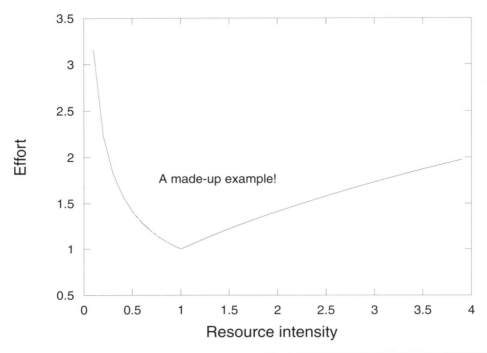

(Quantities normalized to their optimum values)

Effort vs. *Resource intensity* — A made-up example!

for a specific task. The goal should be to discover the optimum effort and hence the optimum duration. For example, if away from the optimum, one might discover that a slight increase of resources to a particular task reduces the effort as well as the duration.

Thus, the problem of integrating costs and schedule is complicated because task effort (not just duration) and hence cost depend intrinsically on resource allocation. Initially, a project should be planned with all lowest-level DWBS elements at their optimum durations because this criterion minimizes the costs of individual tasks. However, there is no guarantee that the total project cost is minimized. A project is by definition a complex system, and crashing the right task (i.e., reducing its planned duration by increasing its resources above the optimum) on the critical path may shorten the project's duration sufficiently so that other, more general costs are reduced, lowering the overall cost of the project. Still, the first design of the project should have all elements at their optimum durations, and the project team should understand this concept before undertaking the next important step: a bottom-up integration.

A Bottom-Up Integration: Map the DWBS onto the RBS

Deriving the project cost from the work packages at the lowest levels of the DWBS (i.e., at the bottom of a graphic representation) entails the most time-consuming budget process, but potentially also the most accurate ("potentially" because this method depends on honest and accurate cost estimates, which reflect the integrity and maturity of the organization).

Other types of budgeting processes may require less work in the short run (and may also be used to complement this method), but a project manager who understands this prescription can rely on it confidently. Further, estimating efforts should focus on the elements that make the project more of a project and less of a process.

Work, loosely defined, fills a spectrum from process to project. "Process" implies routine; machines and people execute familiar and well-understood tasks repeatedly, with certainty. As tasks become less familiar, the level of uncertainty rises, as does the importance of contingencies, risk analysis, and any prior knowledge that can provide guidance (i.e., knowledge management).

Although by definition a project always delivers something new, the tasks within it can range across the spectrum from familiar to fresh: from process-type to project-type. At some point in the spectrum, when the feeling about delivering a specific DWBS element crosses some threshold from confident to (very!) concerned, the project team is working with the true project elements.

Similarly, one can say that projects themselves range across a spectrum from producing something only slightly new to creating some object or concept that redefines the state of the art. If the spectrum of tasks runs from process-type to project-type, how should the spectrum of projects be described? Continuing with this line of thinking, one can argue that a project generates anxiety partly as a function of the number of its tasks that are new—that is, as a function of the project's project-type tasks. (More precisely, this concern is probably a function of the number of new tasks per unit time.) No matter how complicated, a project whose individual tasks require little or no new thinking will be tamed fairly easily by good organization and management.

This type of project is much less feared than one whose successful completion depends on devising schemes to solve never-before-encountered problems, that is, where the essential work is at or beyond the state of the art.

"Intensity" is perhaps more appropriately substituted for "anxiety." The notion of a project's intensity depends in some way on the number of totally new tasks contained within the work packages at the lowest levels of the deliverable work breakdown structure. Because the project itself introduces multiple interdependencies with respect to these tasks, the arguments applied to communication nodes suggest that the project's intensity rises as the square of the number of new tasks.

A project with only process-type tasks defines the lowest-intensity project. Normalizing to that scale, Figure 3-4 indicates how the intensity might rise with the number of new tasks. It was produced by saying, arbitrarily, that the intensity of a project with only two truly new tasks is twice that of a similar project with no new tasks, i.e., two fully project-type tasks compared with tasks that lie at the process end of the process-project work spectrum. Independent of where one places this doubling point, the non-linear dependence postulated shows that the project's intensity rises rapidly. Intense projects demand better integration and knowledge management.

For example, in a mature project organization, a solid communications infrastructure will relieve the burden of estimating the routine elements (process-type) through historical knowledge conveyed smoothly to the project team. (As noted earlier, this need ties project management to the concept of managing knowledge.) The reduced burden of routine estimation allows the project team to focus its thinking on the project-type elements.

The RBS contains the cost rates, which have unit dimensions of money per time per resource (e.g., dollars per hour per worker, dollars per week per bulldozer). The dimensions carry through all calculations, and thus the dimensions remaining at the end of any arithmetic manipulations can act as a check on the validity of the calculation. As noted previously, effort, with dimensions of resource times time (e.g., worker hours, bulldozer weeks), multiplied by the cost rate, gives cost.

After determining the costs of the individual elements at the lowest levels of the DWBS, the project team can sum the costs of the DWBS elements up through the various levels of the breakdown structure until the number at the top yields the total project cost. The only actual estimating occurs for the lowest elements; the rest is simply addition.

If the organization has a good RBS and the project team has created a complete DWBS, project planning is off to a great start, and future changes

FIGURE 3-4   Project Intensity As a Function of New Tasks

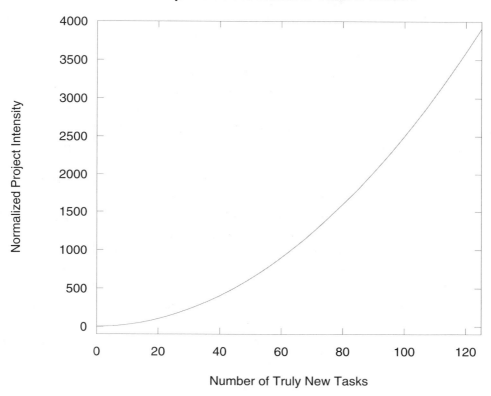

Does Project Intensity Increase with the Square of the Number of New Tasks?

(x-axis) Number of Truly New Tasks

(y-axis) Normalized Project Intensity

in project plans will be much easier to integrate. Now that costs and scope have been determined, schedule remains. Scheduling begins with building the network.

Managing a Network of Elements

Ideally, the WBS shows deliverables at all levels, even the lowest. Implicitly included in the lowest levels are work packages. Work packages can be assigned to individual workers, managers, management teams, or subcontractors, depending on the size of the project. As noted, these elements contain the detailed project activities.

If the implicit tasks are sufficiently well understood, the lowest-level DWBS elements themselves can be used to build the project's network. When displayed as a chart, the network diagram (sometimes referred to misleadingly as a PERT diagram) shows the temporal precedence of the elements: On which element does a given element depend for its start or completion? In other words, which element or elements must precede the given element? Which can then succeed it?

Relationships can be more sophisticated than finish-start, and loops may even be employed (e.g., one repeats work until a product or process passes a test). Two important points must be noted. First, these dependencies are the only constraints preventing all elements from being worked on in parallel. Parallel work is the default in a project—it should not be (with the exception of fast tracking) an efficiency suddenly discovered later. Given sufficient resources (and at this stage of planning, these are assumed), the project team attempts to maximize the number of parallel elements in the network.

Second, a piece of crucial advice accompanies this crucial planning step: Treat the creation of the project's network as a team management exercise, not as an individual software exercise. This task should not be assigned to the bright individual who happens to be the local expert on the network section of the company's favorite project management software. Although modern software does make the mechanics of building the network relatively easy, building the network remains an important process that encourages team integration. The various managers should agree on the order in which project elements must be created. As the number of elements grows, the possibilities of interaction become myriad. Leadership, teamwork, and judgment are called for.

The consequences of a poorly designed first network (iteration is almost always necessary) will become evident quickly once the project enters the execution stage. Unless the project develops perfectly according to the project plans, a poorly designed network will quickly and strongly limit the management flexibility essential to controlling the project.

A Schedule from the DWBS and the Network Diagram

At this stage in project planning, the network diagram and the DWBS (supported by the RBS) drive the schedule calculation. The project team obtains the minimum efforts for all tasks from a combination of historical precedence and the team's own analysis, which in the case of a totally new task may be characterized as a best guess.

Next, the minimum efforts divided by the optimum resource intensities, if understood, give the optimum durations. At this juncture, a brief digression describes the Program Evaluation and Review Technique (PERT), which uses, instead of one deterministic time, three different estimates of a given task's duration. PERT includes estimates of the "optimistic," "pessimistic," and "most likely" durations, where "optimistic" and "pessimistic" are defined in terms of percentages: The best time occurs, say, once in 100 attempts of the same task, and the task's durations are better than the worst 99 times out of that same 100. With the proper assumption about the distribution of these three times, one can obtain probabilistic estimates of a project's scheduled duration and thus provide more complete information to the client (e.g., "There's a 75 percent chance we can finish in 6 months, but a 90 percent chance we can finish in 7 months.") Whether one uses PERT or not, the idea of the three times is worth remembering.

In addition to containing the cost rates that permitted the budget calculation, the RBS also includes the limits on available resources. Ideally, a modern enterprise resource-tracking system might list these limits in essentially real time, based on daily resource use by all other projects in the organization. In the best of all worlds, the organization's resources would permit the optimum duration for all tasks. If the system cannot provide sufficient resources for optimum durations, the costs may increase, the durations will lengthen, and the project team should decide how to distribute the resources most efficiently.

The first integrated project plan is now at hand. The project team has already constructed the precedence-successor relationships in building the network. The team puts the durations into the network and thus creates the first project schedule. Because the project team has already estimated the costs of all DWBS elements, a cost schedule—that is, cost as a function of time—has also effectively been created. But the total plan is still incomplete.

PLANNING FOR MONITORING, EVALUATION, AND CONTROL

During project execution, the team will attempt to maintain integration and meet the triple constraint. To accomplish this goal, the team will monitor the project to determine its progress with respect to the first plans. The expenditures of funds and the completion of tasks will be monitored first. The team will evaluate the monitoring measures and decide whether to take any actions designed to bring the actual project's progress into alignment with the project plan. This alignment process is formally called "control." Planning for this cycle of monitoring, evaluation, and control (analogous to air-traffic control) should begin as soon as the initial schedule has taken shape because the team can then build the monitoring into the schedule.

Too often, monitoring measurements can be represented by the now-standard cartoon of the man looking for his car keys under the lamp post. When asked if he lost them in this area, the man replies "no, but that's where the light is."

For a real example, take the old conglomerate AT&T before it was broken apart. In an attempt to measure operating efficiency, massive amounts of statistics were compiled monthly into a telephone book–sized volume, "Ma Bell's Green Book." From month to month, little of the data changed significantly. A senior official reportedly related that the process alone was worthwhile because it kept the operating companies "on their toes." [21]

The project team can maintain the focus on project integration by emphasizing an integrated viewpoint in the design of the project's monitoring. In Chapter 5, on project implementation, we examine a particular integration scheme (earned-value analysis), but for now let's review the planning process and the criteria for good measurements.

Understanding Good Measurements

Words have common, everyday understandings that often differ from their use in technical fields. When lawyers use "assault" in a legal proceeding, for example, they use it as a "term of art": it has a specific meaning in its technical context. In physics, "velocity" has a specific meaning, and it carries more information than "speed." Often words' everyday meanings are insufficiently precise, and misunderstandings can hinder performance for two reasons: (1) agreement is impossible without a common understanding, and (2) the precise meaning informs and even directs. Such is the case for the terminology useful in project selection models and, by extension, for monitoring.

In everyday speech, people often use the word "objective" to denote opinions or measurements made by fair, disinterested observers (us), in contrast to the subjective measurements and opinions of prejudiced people (them). "Objective" is therefore often meant as a synonym for "good." Thus, a project management instructor was once observed to say, with the students echoing the refrain, that "subjective" measurements are "bad." Not so.

As a term of art, "objective" means that the standards to which one compares the measurement are external to the individual or system making the measurement, so others can see the standards; subjective measures use internal standards. Baseball's strike zone provides an excellent example. The rule book describes objectively the volume through which the ball must pass to meet the definition of a strike. In practice, however, each individual baseball umpire interprets the rule differently, creating a subjective strike zone. (Interestingly, a consistent subjective strike zone on the part of an individual umpire allows players to gain knowledge of its true dimensions; it thus becomes, at least in some informal sense, objective.)

Managers earn their pay through good judgment, and so subjective monitoring measurements, based on the experience of the manager or delegated team members, should not be avoided unreasonably. As illustrated in the AT&T example, projects sometimes become obsessed with objective standards because of the relative ease of obtaining information, whether or not the information brings valid understanding of the project's progress. In contrast, art and antique experts make many subjective measurements, and large amounts of money change hands based on these judgments.

Project management experts can be similarly well-educated and knowledgeable, and their opinions—subjective though they may be—should also be respected. Returning once from reviewing a project, a senior scientist at NASA headquarters reported his certainty that a project team could not complete a spacecraft's software by the deadline. He did not have objective criteria (possibly neither did the team members), but having written much software himself, he had the subjective sense that optimism was overriding better judgments, and ultimately he was proven correct.

"Quantitative" and "qualitative" suffer from a misunderstanding similar to that between "objective" and "subjective." Simply put, quantitative measurements add and qualitative ones do not. Given two houses, adding their interior floor areas yields the total area of the two buildings. If one house is green and one is blue, the addition of these two qualities makes no sense. More subtly, however, adding the average floor area per room in one house to that same quantity from the other house also makes no sense. Those measurements are qualitative.

The tendency is to give greater weight to objective and quantitative measures, but project managers can use properly calibrated subjective and qualitative measurements. In the end, though, the project team should express all measurements numerically. "Good," "better," "slower," "faster," "cheaper," "far," "near," and, perhaps most difficult, "about" should be transformed into numbers, if necessary using the proverbial "on a scale of 1 to 10...." For example, although red, yellow, and green lights are currently quite popular, when the lights are transformed into 1s, 2s, and 3s, one recognizes their limited resolution.

The project manager needs reliable measurements. Reliable means that if a similar measurement is made of a similar quantity, a similar answer will result. For example, if a team makes length measurements with yardsticks but afterwards discovers the sticks each actually had a length of one meter, the measurements will be wrong but reliable, i.e., repeatable. If the error is subsequently discovered, the measurements can be transformed correctly into the right lengths.

Finally, the measurements must be valid. That is, the measurements must truly reflect what the team intended to measure: The measurements must represent reality. To summarize: measures, whether subjective or objective, quantitative or qualitative, should be "numeric, reliable, and valid." [21]

These measurements, now added to the project plan, cause the first iteration of the just-completed schedule and budget because the team has added effort to its project. The team must account for the resources needed to effect the monitoring; the work breakdown structure will have some new or expanded elements with additional deliverables (monitoring results).

Implementing the Cycle

Project managers earn a good portion of their salaries in evaluation. As part of the cycle of monitoring, evaluation, and control, evaluation includes the decision of whether or not to impose controls on the project. Controlling the project means taking actions to drive the project's progress back into accord with the original plan. The monitoring results are judged, and a decision is made: do nothing; examine more data; control. If one finds a project "out of control" (but not to the extent that termination is the next step), the last alternative is demanded.

Paradoxically, an integrated project without contingencies does not allow for the concept of control, by definition. Contingencies of funds, time, or even performance goals can be considered the global equivalent of the float in individually scheduled activities. One compensates for falling behind in schedule, or overrunning budget, or a probable shortfall in performance by allowing for more time, funds, or other resources to bring the project back on schedule, on budget, or within designated scope parameters. But if one has not planned for any contingencies, the absence of this generic slack will not permit the project to remain within the volume set by the three axes of the original triple constraint.

Who is responsible for this monitoring? The linear responsibility chart lists project tasks or low-level deliverables and those responsible for their accomplishment. The project team builds a matrix by showing a level of the DWBS along the left-hand column and the project organizational breakdown across the top row. (The OBS breaks down the organizational structure in much the same way that the DWBS delineates the deliverables.) At the column intersections, one lists the specific responsibility assigned. Typically these indicate overall responsibility or responsibility for support, notification, or approval. One could add "integration" as a category.

The integration category would not appear for all tasks but would appear explicitly in all monitoring activities. The person responsible for integration would explain the consequences of a problem in terms of cost, schedule, and scope. Implicit in the explanation would be an evaluation of the monitoring results and suggested actions (see Figure 3-5).

During execution, how can the project team realign the actual project with the project plan? The manner of the question presupposes that the project's scope remains fixed. If the client decides to relax this criterion, reducing the scope can immediately transform the schedule and the budget to overcome current delays and cost overruns. However, the project team has not discovered the root causes of the problems that caused the delays and overruns, so this solution works only in the short term.

What else can be tried? The resource distribution can be altered. The project can be fast-tracked (do tasks in parallel that usually are done in sequence) or crashed; schedules can be analyzed and adjusted with techniques such as time impact analysis or as-planned versus as-built comparison. Knowledge of the optimum duration is again important in keeping the project well integrated because moving task durations away from the optimum will increase costs.

AUDITS

The greater team will appreciate the project team's positive attitude toward improving the project's integrated plan. Especially in the development stage, this approach includes listening to outside opinions. Therefore, it includes project management audits.

A project management audit can concentrate on any part of a project's management. Outside project management, the word "audit" is usually associated with financial accounting, and it has a negative connotation, as though automatically implying errors or even malfeasance. In a mature project management environment, the word will carry a more neutral meaning, similar

FIGURE 3–5   Responsibility Chart (with Explicit Integration Role)

Deliverable WBS		Responsibility				
		Project Manager	Contract Administ.	Integrator	Lead Hardware Engineer	Lead Software Engineer
Work Package	Activity					
A) List of Detailed Specifications		A	R	S	N	N
	A1	S		N	R	N
	A2	S		N	N	R
B) Deliverable WBS		R	A	N	S	S
C) Monitoring Plan		R	N	A	S	S
	C1	S		S	R	N
	C2	S		S	N	R
D) Risk Plan		R	N	A	S	S
	D1	S		S	R	N
	D2	S		S	N	R
	D3	R		A	S	S

Responsible, Approve, Support, Notified: R, A, S, N

perhaps to an examination in the sense of a medical examination: The audit will check the health of a project. In the most sophisticated (mature?) environments, the word will imply welcome assistance to improve a project.

The Early Audit Catches the Worm

When should audits occur? Early. One study found that audits produce maximum value when they occur at 25 percent of the development phase! [21] This criterion suggests that if you were participating in a project that anticipated four days of project management design, at the end of the first day you should stand up and say, "Great job—let's bring in an audit team first thing tomorrow." Even in the best of organizations, this good idea will take some getting used to.

The benefit of the audit is proportional to the timely utilization of the audit's results. During the development phase, unless the audit team concludes that total ineptitude on the part of the project team precludes its continuing, the audit team's analysis should go to the project team, allowing it to sharpen the project plan. Audit results during the implementation phase should assist the PM in controlling the project, i.e., in taking the actions necessary to bring the project's budget and schedule into agreement with the baseline project plan. Post-project audits will find their way to the organization's project management office to aid future project planning. As with monitoring, audits occurring during the implementation phase should be planned into the project's schedule.

A New Type of Audit?

But why discuss audits in the context of integration? As noted, a project management audit can focus on any or all aspects of the project's plans or implementation, be they technical or of human management. In the absence of an isolated, specific problem that demands examination, focusing the audit on integration alone may yield the best results.

While the audit can also examine the integration of project team and greater team personnel, the integration audit team will direct its efforts primarily toward examining the fundamental consistency of the project plans *vis à vis* the triple constraint, to the seeming disregard of everything else. But because integration management is project management, an integration audit becomes, in fact, the most basic type of project audit possible.

The auditors will examine the project's now well-defined scope, its anticipated schedule, and its detailed budget. Just as the project manager set the tone for the team's initial planning, the auditors can look for the right attitude regarding integration. Do the project team members consider all three areas of the triple constraint when they speak of the project, or do they consistently speak only of one or two, neglecting the remaining two or one?

Then the auditors go to the top of the DWBS, where they will look at the major deliverables and their relationship to each other in the milestone network. Do the milestone deliverables reflect a proper understanding of the project's scope, and does the network dictate a reasonable progression?

How were the costs of the DWBS elements determined? Was an effort made to determine minimum efforts and use optimum durations? Do the individual costs of the DWBS elements sum to the total project cost? Are these costs consistent with the durations of the planned schedule? Are the durations consistent with the scope of the project? Are the durations realistic, that is, given the available resources, are the durations doable? Is the resource distribution as a function of time manageable?

The auditors may also want to understand how the project team would keep the project integrated when faced with project changes. The auditors can ask to see the process by which the team would answer hypothetical questions, such as: If the client demands that the total duration of the project be shortened by 17 percent, how will the scope and budget change? After 31 percent of the schedule has been completed as planned, how will the schedule and budget be affected by a 13 percent reduction in scope? How would the team respond if the client demanded an increase in scope of 11 percent with no change in the original project duration?

By focusing on the triple constraint and assessing the project team's understanding of an integrated project, the auditors will learn much, if not all, of what they need to know to understand the reality of the project's plan, even at an early stage of the development phase. The inherent requirement of a well-integrated project, which perhaps seems obvious to those studying project management, is violated to an extreme extent in the real world, as the following two examples show.

After hiding cost overruns and schedule delays for more than a year, and despite a total of 11 management or science reviews that found little wrong, the National Ignition Facility, a critical post–Cold War project at the Department of Energy's Lawrence Livermore National Laboratory, was forced to double both its budget (to approximately $4 billion) and its scheduled duration. Shortly before the new budget numbers were announced, a study team called the project one of the best managed they had ever seen. [34]

The National Aeronautics and Space Administration (NASA) had some well-publicized planetary-probe failures that prompted a reexamination of its so-called faster, better, cheaper approach. At the highest levels, NASA officials finally realized that if cost, scope, and schedule remain rigid, only risk will grow.

But the hard workers at DOE and NASA deserve much respect, and certainly many seasoned project managers must have recognized the problems before they grew so big. Thus, not only must project managers be educated about integration, but so must the members of the greater teams, including—and maybe especially—those toward the top of the organizational hierarchy.

THE CONTRACT AS AN INTEGRATING MECHANISM

The project manager and the core project team should be brought into project planning before the contract is signed. Then, instead of viewing the contract as a necessary evil, complete with dark villains (lawyers), an enthusiastic (and tireless) project team will see the contract as the final integrating mechanism of the project's development stage. Before the first construction drawing is made or the first line of code is written, the contract allows the project team to solidify its integrated vision of the project's implementation. The team will probably have spent a long time planning, and the project manager must contain the team's eagerness to move the project forward into reality. The project team should not forgo an opportunity to influence the contract. It could even consider asking the opinions of the greater team.

The project manager should demand that the contract be written in plain English, so that humans can understand it—good lawyers will do so without such an exhortation. The lawyers in turn should depend on the project manager's expertise to ensure that the contract does not separate the project's scope from its budget and schedule. This requirement translates into heavy involvement on the part of the manager, who must examine carefully the contract's statement of work, payment clauses, and milestone dates. On a long or expensive project, the funding planning must also fit the project planning: Will the funds be available when resource needs are greatest?

From the integration perspective, how will the team and the client handle the inevitable changes that occur as a project progresses? The modification provisions in the contract could, for example, include a requirement that all requested alterations be manifested formally in all three areas of the triple constraint, even if the initiators of the change expect (magically) to cause only an isolated modification.

Understanding that the goal of an integrated project is meeting the triple constraint, the project manager should help produce a contract that permits both sides to benefit from project improvements suggested by either side. Again in the spirit of integration, if both client and contractor can benefit, each has incentive to strengthen the project.

This flexibility may encourage creative solutions to the problems that will inevitably arise during implementation. For example, where possible, insist on functional specifications (i.e., not design or performance specs). By allowing easier tradeoffs among budget, schedule, and scope, functional specifications improve the chances of solving problems within the general bounds of the original integrated triple constraint.

A good contract helps avoid disputes during the project. It may also prevent future litigation, especially if records are maintained. A consistently integrated perspective in these records will minimize factual disagreement between client and contractor because budget, schedule, and scope will all have been addressed.

In short, a good contract helps enforce good management and can motivate good planning. As a reminder of the process that a team should follow in developing its plans and managing its project, Figure 3-6 presents a path toward an integrated project.

FIGURE 3-6 A Process for Developing an Integrated Project

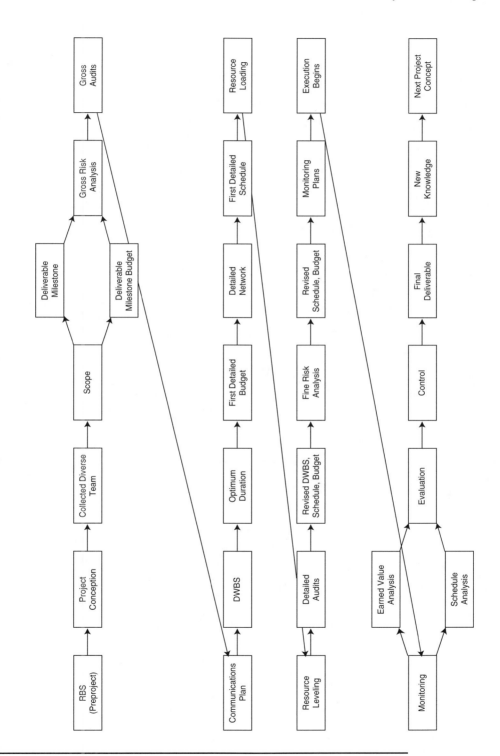

CHAPTER 4

Execution and Closeout

T he execution of a project begins when the so-called real work begins, but two important, related issues should be understood. First, because project phases overlap, beginning implementation does not imply that planning has ceased. Second, control requires action beyond what the original plans have specified for project execution; this control, as described in Chapter 3, should follow monitoring and evaluation during execution. As noted, the project team builds the monitoring–evaluation–control cycle into the project plan.

But how does one measure and evaluate the project's progress in an integrated manner? The mechanics come in the method called earned-value analysis. The old computer maxim GIGO (garbage in, garbage out) holds here too, and whether an earned-value analysis yields useful, valid results depends, as always, on the judgments of the project team. Good judgments and subsequent actions transform earned-value analysis into earned-value management.

EARNED-VALUE ANALYSIS

Earned-value analysis is a tool for examining the integration of cost, schedule, and scope during and after the execution of a project. While it is a potentially powerful integrating mechanism, however, EVA may not indicate the requisite controls for several reasons:

1. Although recently improved by the Project Management Institute (PMI®), the still-awkward notation makes manipulation of the variables difficult for the inexperienced, and understanding is hindered. [25]
2. The linear determinism of the analysis makes predictions problematic.
3. Values are often not decided disinterestedly in the planning stage.

An alternative notation makes formal manipulations easier to follow. In this new notation, the inversion of a couple of traditional indices increases the tool's utility. Also, a manager can present a single number to estimate a project's integrated progress.

Understanding Earned Value: Evolving the Notation Beyond PMBOK®

A project finishes with some delivery, at some cost, at some specific time, and the project team can compare these end points to the project's original baseline. But how does one quantify a project's progress in an integrated manner before it ends? At a finer scale, how does one quantify the progress of an activity within the project? One answer lies in the original definition of earned value: the budgeted cost of work performed. Note immediately the commonsense approach of limning only those activities that have been performed. Of course, how one measures the amount of work performed, even within a single activity, takes some thought. In this ultimately business-like approach, the earned value is measured in cost; its unit is the currency's unit.

The other two quantities essential to earned-value analysis also are defined in terms of cost. Again using the pre-PMBOK® 2000 terminology, we have the actual cost of the work performed and the budgeted cost of the work scheduled. A generation of project managers learned to use these concepts through the four initials of the defining phrases.

The second concept, the actual cost, is in principle the easiest of the three to determine: The accountants relate the cost of the work performed. The third quantity, the budgeted cost of the work scheduled, comes directly from the plans: At any given time, how much money would have been spent if the plans had been followed perfectly?

Anyone who has taught EVA knows that the awkwardness of the old four-letter shorthands creates difficulty in learning and using earned-value analysis. (As Frame writes, "the students spend more time trying to master the vocabulary than the concepts." [13]) One can infer that the Project Management Institute also understood some of these problems, because in the latest revision to the PMBOK®, PMI® (encouraged by other institutions) changed the designations. The PMBOK® now suggests using simply "earned value" for the budgeted cost of work performed. This equivalence derives directly from the definition, which must continue to live because "earned value" conveys no meaning in itself; one must remember "budgeted cost of work performed" to understand the concept.

For "actual cost of work performed," PMBOK® suggests dropping the "work performed," leaving "actual cost." This change improves the description. Ideally, one would have costs only for work performed, but sometimes one pays for work that is, for good reasons or bad, incomplete at the time of payment. Nevertheless, one still has paid for it, and this new term is unambiguous.

For "budgeted cost of work scheduled," however, PMBOK® suggests "planned value," which naturally leads to two questions: (1) Of what? and (2) Exactly what is value, and how is it measured? Again, one is forced to return to the original definition. The suggested abbreviations for these new definitions are EV, PV, and AC.

If project management is part art and part science, why not use the tools of science where they improve comprehension and clarity? A definition and its corresponding notation need not have one-to-one alphabetic correspondence. Use as many words as necessary to define the concepts, but make the notation as compact as possible so that it can be manipulated easily. Scientists generally do not manipulate four-letter abbreviations (the old earned-value terminology), and algebraic scientific notation, although often burdened with history, seeks to communicate information, not mask it. The following consistent, single-letter notation for the three earned-value parameters is therefore proposed (the old four-letter abbreviations are listed in parentheses after the new terminology):

C_b: Earned value (BCWP)
C_s: Planned value (BCWS)
C_a: Actual cost (ACWP)

The shorthand notation reads easily as "budgeted cost," "scheduled cost," and "actual cost."

Figure 4-1 presents a standard portrayal of earned-value parameters, with new notation. Instead of "planned," the subscript s is used for schedule because schedule is a narrower, more precise word; every aspect of a project is (should be) planned, but not every part is scheduled. The figure, for a fictional project, illustrates the three earned-value costs at 80 percent of the original scheduled completion. Note that only the scheduled costs go to 100 percent.

This notation has several immediate advantages. First, the measure of the values as costs is indicated immediately through the letter C. Second, the three costs are defined clearly by the subscripts on the Cs: budgeted, scheduled, and actual. Further, this notation extends to the cost and schedule differences, ΔC_a and ΔC_s, respectively, which may now be defined in a consistent manner, with one equation, $\Delta C_i \equiv C_b - C_i$, where $i = a$ or s; the two individual forms are:

FIGURE 4–1   Earned Value Parameters

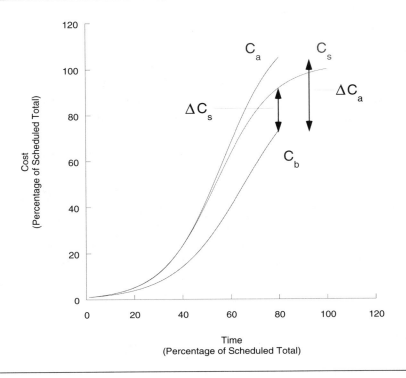

$$\Delta C_a \equiv C_b - C_a \qquad (4.1a)$$
$$\Delta C_s \equiv C_b - C_s. \qquad (4.1b)$$

"Difference" is better than "variance" (the usual term) because it communicates more precisely the operation being performed. The statistical implications of the word "variance" are nowhere to be found in these subtractions: ΔC_a and ΔC_s each gives the difference between two quantities.

In the first equation, the difference between the budgeted cost of the accomplished work and the actual cost of the work performed reflects the project's performance with respect to budget. In the second case, when the scheduled cost is subtracted from the budgeted cost, an indication of performance with respect to schedule is obtained. In either case, a positive difference tells a team that its project is proceeding better than planned; a negative difference indicates problems.

Typically, the earned value (C_b) is normalized to the actual cost (C_a) to produce an efficiency factor referred to as the "cost performance index"; a similar normalization to the scheduled cost (C_s) would yield the "schedule performance index." A number greater than one indicates a project performing at a higher level than planned.

However, as Anbari pointed out some years ago, one obtains more useful quantities if the indices are instead inverted. [2] To differentiate from the usual definitions ("indices"), denote these new quantities as the (actual) cost performance factor:

$$F_a \equiv \frac{C_a}{C_b},$$ (4.2a)

and the schedule performance factor:

$$F_s \equiv \frac{C_s}{C_b}.$$ (4.2b)

One may improve the overall project extrapolation by combining data from many project tasks. The individual factors from the individual tasks could be added and averaged, but that method would give equal weight to tasks of vastly different magnitude. Instead, the average factors are given by the sums of the actual and scheduled costs divided by the sum of the budgeted costs. The summations occur over the number of tasks, N, that have been completed or are in progress at some point in the execution of the project. The formal definitions of the aggregate (or cumulative) cost factor, $\bar{F}_a$, and the aggregate schedule factor, $\bar{F}_s$, are simply:

$$\bar{F}_a \equiv \sum_{j=1}^{N}(C_a)_j \div \sum_{j=1}^{N}(C_b)_j$$ (4.3a)

$$\bar{F}_s \equiv \sum_{j=1}^{N}(C_s)_j \div \sum_{j=1}^{N}(C_b)_j.$$ (4.3b)

To be able to think of an average factor, $\bar{F}_a$ or $\bar{F}_s$, in terms of its individual components, $(F_a)_j \equiv (C_a)_j \div (C_b)_j$ or $(F_s)_j \equiv (C_s)_j \div (C_b)_j$, is possible with the new definition of a weighting factor, w_j, for each individual cost or schedule factor:

$$w_j \equiv (C_b)_j \div \sum_{k=1}^{N}(C_b)_k.$$ (4.4)

As above, the sum, $\sum_{k=1}^{N}\left(C_b\right)_k$, is over all terms. For any given earned-value calculation, it is a constant that need only be calculated once. The weighting factors themselves sum to unity:

$$\sum_{j=1}^{N} w_j = 1. \tag{4.5}$$

The weighting factor, as the name implies, gives the proportional importance of any given F_a or F_s compared to the other individual factors. It is a way of formalizing what should be obvious: The larger the budgeted cost of the work performed (i.e., the earned value), the more important the factor. The larger the factor, the more attention it should receive, especially if it becomes greater than one.

With this weighting factor, the average factors can be written in terms of the individual factors:

$$\bar{F}_a = \sum_{j=1}^{N} w_j (F_a)_j \tag{4.6a}$$

$$\bar{F}_s = \sum_{j=1}^{N} w_j (F_s)_j. \tag{4.6b}$$

For ease of notation in the descriptions that follow, the earned value of an individual task will be portrayed without loss of generality; aggregate values can easily be substituted via the above formalism.

Possibilities in Predictions

The above F factors can be used to attempt to predict future performance based on past performance. Basic EVA makes the bold assumption that the extrapolation of the project's schedule and costs will proceed linearly—that is, with respect to the project plans, schedule and cost will evolve just as they have earlier in the project. Before proceeding with the simple arithmetic, however, a brief note about the difficulties and concerns with such predictions is warranted.

Determining how much work has been accomplished, i.e., determining the earned value itself, continues to be one of the most difficult problems in EVA. For the calculations to have real meaning, the project team must decide prior to execution how it will measure the budgeted cost of work performed, C_b, for any given task. Our linear minds often have difficulty with an accurate portrayal of this concept. From experience we know that often the last 10 percent of the work takes as long as the first 90 percent. How, then, will value be allocated?

Several simple algorithms have been proposed that have as their advantage consistency more than any claim to accuracy. For example, one could assign half the budgeted cost to a task upon its inception, with the remaining 50 percent to be awarded at completion. More conservatively, one could award 100 percent only at task completion. Given historical data, the progression of a task as a function of time might be known, and then the earned value could also be assigned as a function of time. But even if this problem of allocating value is solved satisfactorily, difficulties remain.

As noted with every advertisement for investing in securities (stocks), past performance does not guarantee future returns. To continue with a financial analogy, the consumer price index uses a "representative basket of goods and services" to estimate inflation. That is, the average increase in the costs of the contents of an average "basket" is extrapolated to the whole economy. Similarly, earned value extrapolates the average performances of project tasks either completed or underway to the remaining project activities. However, no equivalent "basket" of project activities has been defined, and thus there is no guarantee that the tasks on which the earned values are based represent the tasks that remain. For example, in a project containing much construction, the initial set of activities might include much pouring of cement, after which interiors are built. Earned value based on concrete production would probably tell you little about painting walls. Or for a software project, the work in the initial coding of software is of a different nature than the debugging and integration that will follow.

Earned value does not include learning that occurs on the job. It also does not include factors outside the project that can alter future costs, such as political unrest that affects the production of some necessary material, or weather. But factors such as these are considered in risk analysis. The real question is the cost versus the benefit of doing a good earned-value calculation, which is one of the many judgments to be made by the project manager. For all its faults, earned value contributes more to understanding the progress of a project than do the typically subjective analyses seen in many projects ("I think we're 10 percent behind schedule"), and some form of it is generally recommended to assist in maintaining an integrated project.

Those accustomed to the standard definitions are asked to make a mental adjustment: The project is performing better than expected when the *F* factors are less than one, and the project is underperforming when the *F* factors are greater than one. The improved utility of these definitions is demonstrated in two ways: (1) they become multiplicative factors, instead of divisors; and (2) the percentage increase in the project's cost or schedule is produced by a simple subtraction of 1. (If you do not wish to change definitions that are now effectively hardwired into your brain, you can substitute $1/F$ for F in the following equations.)

Use the subscript 1 to indicate the end of a project, and a prime ($'$) to denote a quantity extrapolated, before the project's end, from the current earned-value numbers. With this notation, one new estimate of the total project duration, $\Delta T_1'$, in terms of the originally scheduled project duration, ΔT_1, is given as:

$$\Delta T_1' = \Delta T_1 F_s. \tag{4.7}$$

The similar estimate of the total project cost is given by:

$$C_{a,1}' = C_{s,1} F_a, \tag{4.8}$$

where $C_{s,1}$ indicates the original estimate of the total project cost at completion, and again the subscript a represents the actual cost. At the time of the earned-value measurements, then, the estimate of the cost needed to complete the project is $\delta C' = C_{a,1}' - C_a.$

Note that these estimates assume that the project's entire duration and cost will scale as did the activities from which the earned values have been obtained. Other algorithms are possible, of course. These would depend on what assumptions one would like to make about the performance of the remaining tasks in terms of the performance of the completed or in-progress tasks. The extremes range from assuming completely equivalent efficiency, as above, to assuming that the remainder of the project will proceed as originally planned (which, in the absence of some compelling reasons, would be, to put it most kindly, overly optimistic). One could also assume that future efficiency will be worse. In any case, the equations that follow continue with the assumption of complete equivalence.

The difference between the current estimate and the original estimate of the final project cost would be:

$$\Delta C_1' = C_{a,1}' - C_{s,1}. \tag{4.9}$$

With this definition, a positive cost difference shows that more will have to be spent than originally planned; a negative difference means that the current estimate is less than the original estimate. This cost difference can be expressed in terms of the project's original estimate of the total cost, which is identical to the scheduled cost at the end of the project, $C_{s,1}$:

$$\frac{\Delta C_1'}{C_{s,1}} = F_a - 1. \qquad (4.10a)$$

The corresponding calculation for the total project duration yields:

$$\frac{\Delta T_1'}{\Delta T_1} = F_s - 1. \qquad (4.10b)$$

Again, if the differences are less than zero (if the factors are less than one), the project is performing better than originally planned. These definitions can be generalized to the change from the original estimate of any planned cost or duration:

$$\frac{\Delta C'}{C_s} = F_a - 1, \qquad (4.11a)$$

$$\frac{\Delta T'}{\Delta T_s} = F_s - 1, \qquad (4.11b)$$

where C' and $\Delta T'$ represent any (future) cost or duration, and C_s and ΔT_s represent the cost or duration originally scheduled. If the project is underperforming, these quantities are positive: For any given future task, as well as for the complete project, the project will require funds and time in excess of the original estimate by a percentage $100(F_a - 1)$ and $100(F_s - 1)$, respectively; if the factor is less than 1, the negative result shows savings of cost or time.

The integration of cost and schedule gives the earned-value technique its power, and the inverse index formalism used here yields the possibility of another quantity not anticipated by Anbari. Because the two factors have a common denominator (the earned value), they can be added directly to derive a single number that indicates the health of a project.

The goal in this definition is to have a quantity that behaves in the same manner as the separate factors, that is, to have one number that can produce, when necessary, an unambiguous warning about the integrated project performance. And so define a new quantity, the cost–schedule performance factor, with the (uppercase) Greek letter Φ, as:

$$\Phi \equiv F_a + F_s - 1 + \sqrt{\frac{1}{2}(F_a - F_s)^2}, \qquad (4.12)$$

where the last term accounts for the spread about the mean value of F_a and F_s; the square root of the square is retained to emphasize that the absolute value of the difference is needed. Without this term, a low F_a, for example, could hide a high F_s. On the other hand, if the separate cost and schedule factors track each other identically, which says that the project is proceeding as planned—in some ways at least—this term adds nothing. As with the individual performance factors, any $\Phi > 1$ shows a project with possible problems. Any project with $\Phi > 1$ should be watched closely (i.e., monitored) and controlled until $\Phi = 1$. The average cost/schedule factor, $\overline{\Phi}$, is calculated by using the two aggregate individual factors, $\overline{F}_a$ and $\overline{F}_s$, respectively.

Some quantity analogous to a percentage increase is given by $\Phi - 1$. Because cost and schedule have been combined, this percentage increase cannot be easily interpreted in terms of cost or schedule separately. Nevertheless, high values warn about total project performance.

The Example of the Widgets

A project plans to deliver six widgets, at a cost of $1 each, in six days. At the end of five days, three widgets have been produced, at a total cost of $4. What does the earned-value analysis say? We have the following equalities:

$$
\begin{aligned}
C_b &= \$3 \\
C_a &= \$4 \\
C_s &= \$5 \\
C_{s,1} &= \$6.
\end{aligned}
\tag{4.13}
$$

The cost difference, $\Delta C_a \equiv C_b - C_a = -\$1$; the project is over budget, as one knew from a simple glance at the numbers. Likewise, it is also behind schedule: $\Delta C_s \equiv C_b - C_s = -\$2$.

How efficiently has the project team used its budget and schedule? In terms of cost, $F_a = C_a/C_b = 1.33$, and in terms of schedule, $F_s = C_s/C_b = 1.67$. In other words, the project spent 33 percent more to accomplish the work that had been budgeted, and 67 percent more, as measured in terms of cost, should have been accomplished.

The new, linear estimate of the actual cost at the end of the project is $C'_{a,1} = C_{s,1} \times F_a = \$8.00$. From this point, $\delta C' = C'_{a,1} - C_a = \$4.00$ more must be spent to complete widget production.

With these calculated, the new linear estimate of the total project duration is $\Delta T'_1 = \Delta T_1 \times F_s = 10$ days. At the end of the project, the cost difference between the plan and the anticipated spending to complete the project will be $\Delta C'_1 = C'_{a,1} - C_{s,1} = \$2.00$.

The total performance of the project is summarized by calculating the cost/schedule performance factor, $\Phi = F_a + F_s - 1 + \sqrt{\left((F_s - F_a)^2/2\right)} = 2.24$. The variance term, $\left(\sqrt{(F_s - F_a)^2/2}\right)$, reflects the difference between the two indices and adds 0.24. In any case, we can safely say that in terms of its current cost and schedule, the project will require greater than 100 percent more combined time and resources.

PROJECT CLOSEOUT AND A GLOBAL TRANSITION TO EVM

Finishing a project presents a last opportunity to examine the project's integration, and an organization with a mature project management culture will provide the resources. (One might argue that a lack of closeout reports and analyses means a project was not integrated at the end, despite what may have occurred earlier in its life.) If the project was carried out in an organization with a project management office, the office should recognize the importance of pinning down the position of the project in the volume defined by the three axes of the triple constraint, and an integration scorecard can be created. How?

Some subset of the project team, along with representatives of the organization's project management office, can create a complete earned-value analysis of the project as seen throughout its history. This new team can judge the effectiveness of the earned-value analyses performed throughout the project at say, every 20 percent of its completion (20, 40, 60, 80, and 100 percent), or every 10 percent, or every month, or every day. How good were the predictions when the project was 20 percent complete as compared to the predictions made at 40 percent complete? (History tends to show that if a project is far behind early, the dismal earned-value prediction is, unfortunately, accurate.) What about at 60 percent? Did some project activities show the tendency for their remaining 10 percent to take as long as the first 90 percent? From such an analysis, the predictive power of EVA can be sharpened.

As is always the case in closeout reports, the two key questions are: (1) What did we learn? and (2) How can we do better? This post-facto analysis obviously does not affect the progress of the just-completed project. For that project, the earned-value analysis remains merely a part of the post-mortem, albeit a fundamental part. For future projects within the organization, however, the analysis assists the evolution of earned value from an isolated analysis tool into a real-time management tool: Earned-value *analysis* becomes real earned value *management*.

In the particular context of earned-value analysis, "how can we do better?" may translate into better real-time measurements of the earned value itself before project completion. Here "better" has an explicit meaning: Better measurements have more predictive value.

Perhaps the analysis would reveal that the current measurements methods can predict project progress more accurately by modifying the linear predictions of standard earned value. Maybe, for example, one discovers that for earned-value measurements made at 20 percent of the completion of a project, Equation 4.8, which gives the new estimate of the total project cost, should include an additional multiplicative factor of 12 percent: $C'_{a,1} = (1.12)C_{s,1}F_a$; a different factor might be used at a different project completion fraction.

When done properly, closeout begins the transformation of specific project information to more general knowledge that can be used throughout the organization. With this knowledge, project managers (if they are given the time and resources to acquire and study it!) can do a better job of integrating and managing future projects.

As discussed in Chapter 1, this transformation of local information into organizational knowledge represents an integration itself, in the original sense of Leibniz. The organization takes advantage of its experience with a single project by collecting the data and information produced in the course of the project, analyzing them, and organizing, archiving, and redistributing what has been transformed into knowledge. The process represents a meta-integration of project integration management.

CHAPTER 5

Integrating Personnel and Other Interested Parties

The basic idea of managers and teams is fundamental to human society. Modern project managers understand the need for and value of diverse project teams. But team members must be treated as individuals; freedom is good. Integration presents itself as the answer to some team problems. An organization with a mature, integrative approach will replace the two-dimensional notion of interfaces with three-dimensional spaces of integration.

Although mathematical integration equations are easily written, no simple algorithm comes to mind for project integration. Still, if there were one, project personnel would multiply all other terms, so we are quite correct to call the integration of project personnel a factor. Perfect integration of budget, schedule, and scope will not prevent failure if a project and its personnel are not also integrated. To a lesser extent, the greater team should be integrated too.

"UNIVERSALS OF CULTURE"

Let's begin with a fundamental question: How valid are the widely accepted notions of managers and teams? That is, does another structure exist within which projects could be better integrated?

In a 1945 study, anthropologist George P. Murdock examined descriptions of the social interactions manifest in the hundreds of Earth's societies catalogued at that time. Individualistic managers or workers might be surprised to learn that cooperative labor and division of labor are two of only 67 "universals of culture." [35] The evidence and the arguments are strong that these universals are biologically driven: They are part of what makes us human.

In addition, the renowned (and controversial) expert on organizational dynamics, Elliot Jacques, claims that a hierarchy is not merely a natural way to organize work—it is the best way. [16] This assertion must surprise anyone who, despite all the words about flat organizational structures, has experienced the stifling bureaucracies that are so widespread.

The structural form does not cause these difficulties. They are caused by the rules and the reward systems, formal or otherwise, that determine how people act. Project managers and team members have to see the goal at all times (meeting the triple constraint), feel responsible for it, and do what is necessary to achieve it; rewards should follow.

THE PROJECT TEAM

Integrating people precludes turf wars. A dedicated project manager will attempt to obtain the best people for the project team. For one reason or another, the project might not be able to include them as full members of the team, but the project manager can still seek their opinions, whether regularly and formally (e.g., as paid consultants), or irregularly and informally (e.g., at lunch). Focused on meeting the triple constraint, the good project manager believes "a good idea is a good idea," and its origin is of no concern.

Encouraging Diverse Teams and Healthy Organizations

The best team will almost always be a diverse team, that is, a team diverse in the skills and perspectives of its members. Growing project complexity and increasing international interactions in the 21st century will require more diverse project teams. This diversity will manifest itself in multiple locations, ethnicities, skills, and professional points of view; the latter is a natural outcome of requiring multiple professional disciplines on modern projects.

The collected experience of a diverse team will be far wider than that of a homogenous team. A diverse team potentially will do a better job of determining and integrating possible concerns of the parties at interest. More important, if properly managed, a diverse team will also be more creative. As one author put it so well, this diversity can cause ideas to "combine and combust in exciting and useful ways." [1]

While increasing the potential for improved productivity, this growth of diversity also suggests a rise in the likelihood of conflict. That conflict should be viewed initially as a positive indication that team members feel free to bring different approaches to solving a project's problems. Some approaches will work better than others. Eventually the conflict must disappear as the team coordinates its efforts into an integrated project plan.

While much has been written on team building, Jacques points out that the working contract is a contract between the organization and the individual. Even in professional team sports, contracts deal with individual accomplishments, not the success of the team. And by their very nature, project teams stay complete for at most the one project. The next project will be different, by definition, and it will have a more or less different set of team members. These observations suggest the paradox that the good project manager must treat people as individuals to integrate them with the team and the project.

But in the real world, what evidence would show such integration? One indicator would be if individuals are matched with the right assignments; this is an essential component that establishes an environment conducive to both integration and creativity. [1]

Also, whether as individuals or as members of a team, workers appreciate making contributions and being recognized for them. Integration can improve efficiency if, for example, managers establish an operational mode expressed well in the open-source software culture: "Nobody should ever have to solve a problem twice." This particular attitude moves known task work from project to process, permitting the concentration of intellectual resources on the true project tasks, i.e., the new ones. [10]

The most important attitude in furthering integration may be the implementation of another rule from the open-source culture: "Freedom is good." Freedom enables project personnel to work to their best, and it enables information to flow, which is essential for integration.

While one may associate a lack of freedom with old, well-established organizations, its opposites—suppression and control—can occur anywhere, at any age. Consider the experience of working at one of the many failed dot-coms that was related by a former employee. He reported that his skepticism of the company's potential product was not welcomed. When he asked how the company would make money, silence reigned. He was labeled "negative" for his challenges of the company's direction. His conclusion? "In dot-com land...it was, like, totally uncool to be anything but a cheerleader." [23]

True freedom allows bad news to flow up the chain of command to the people who have the authority to make corrections to control a project or improve a process. Given any competence in the organization, a system with freedom becomes incompatible with managerial incompetence. [10] Therefore, given the involvement of any competent people in a system with communication and freedom, a truly integrated project does not permit sustained incompetence.

Possible Problems

Sometimes the best teams falter. An article subtitled "When Good Teams Go Wrong" discusses one type of problem. [20] A team, working out of sight, develops too strong a self-identity. Because of its initial success, senior management ignores requests for assistance. The team gets further isolated and begins to create its own rules, which it sees as necessary for its continued success. The team deliberately avoids management, and a stalemate ensues, with both sides denying reality.

The author suggests how to prevent this type of problem. Among other things, he says that team personnel and other people from the organization "must be integrated." He goes further, saying that "outside people" should occasionally be brought into the team. Once again we see the importance of an outside perspective, which can be achieved by a continuous process of integrating new people and new knowledge.

Classroom team exercises, designed to show the efficacy of teams over individuals in solving problems, also reveal a disturbing trend. While in most cases a team does better than its average member did alone, a team also often does not do as well as its best individual. In other words, during an attempt to solve a problem, knowledge is available to the organization that it deliberately ignores in favor of other, less advantageous solutions.

Preliminary investigations suggest a possibility that this trend, observed mainly with U.S. students, may have a cultural component. In any case, the preventive medicine for this type of problem is the rule mentioned, "freedom is good." The culture of the organization has to be such that rewards are given both for fighting to bring correct answers out in the open (i.e., talking) and for working well with others to determine which answer is, in fact, the best one (i.e., listening).

SOFTEN INTERFACES

Various types of interfaces exist at a project's many boundaries, both internal and external: between project team members and members of the greater team, between project team members themselves, and between project team members and others in the organization. Organizational interfaces, for example, may get translated into personal ones.

Managers should attempt to go beyond interface management to integration management. An interface refers first to a surface, a two-dimensional boundary that often causes mutual abrasion; an interface is a wall. By extension to the realm of personal connections, interface management can also describe, unfortunately, a two-dimensional (one-dimensional?), shallow relationship. If problems arise, teams based on such relationships will not long survive.

Instead, good project managers need meaningful interactions with people. Meaningful implies the transmission and reception of valid information. Where possible, good managers replace hard surface boundaries with softer, overlapping volumes so both the boundaries and the relationships can now have depth. Project members within—not at—a project boundary will learn about the concerns of the members of the greater team, nominally external to the project. People come together not at an interface but in a finite zone of mutual comfort (see Figure 5-1). In other words, project personnel integrate potentially disruptive outsiders partway into the project. This integration comes only with effort, and therefore with costs that are not to be denied. As discussed more fully in Chapter 6 from a standpoint of power, this integration requires sharing information, as illustrated by the following example.

At the ProjectWorld conference in December 1998, Jan Schlichtmann spoke dramatically of his experiences litigating the toxic-substance case portrayed in the book and the movie, *A Civil Action*. The legal maneuvering

FIGURE 5-1   Turning Interface Management into Integration Management

proved disastrous for all involved, winners and losers alike. Schlichtmann's methods in executing his case ran about as far from good project management principles as one can imagine, but my introductory project management lectures often begin with a story that Schlichtmann related. The story captures the essence of the people side of project integration and illustrates the desired (if here accidental and perhaps temporary) growth from interface management to integration management.

At one point in the case, some long-shut water wells that supplied drinking water were restarted to determine whether contaminated groundwater could have traveled to the wells. One can imagine the chaos of that scene: "...[Schlichtmann] was out on the Aberjona marsh along with an army of a hundred geologists, engineers, hydrologists, well diggers, and lawyers from the EPA, the U.S. Geological Survey, and the environmental consulting firms hired by each of the three parties to the lawsuit." [15]

At ProjectWorld, Schlichtmann described a later meeting with many of these experts to discuss the results of the month-long test. Schlichtmann explained that the technical people were in the audience section of an auditorium, separated physically from the lawyers, who led the discussion up on a stage. Often when a lawyer would claim a certain interpretation of the test results, Schlichtmann noticed that many in the supposedly supporting audience would grimace. The discussions among the lawyers grew more heated, and they left the room to continue their arguments.

When they returned to the room they found the technical people mingling, talking to each other—not concerned so much about who was winning, but in Schlichtmann's words, instead concerned about, and searching for, the truth. They wanted to interpret the data correctly. They wanted to understand. In 2001 Schlichtmann announced the resolution of a similar case, in Toms River, New Jersey, via negotiation, not litigation.

In managing a project, one can impose narrow information conduits across interfaces or instead allow people to communicate with each other directly. Gather all the parties at interest in the same room, whether real or metaphorical, and let them talk to each other. In other words, integrate project personnel and the parties at interest.

CHAPTER 6

Integration and Integrity

ntegration and integrity are inherently related. Both concepts imply wholeness, a prime goal of systemic project management. Integrating a project properly requires communication and freedom. The subsequent sharing of data, information, and knowledge smoothes the distribution of power, enabling good work by all project personnel. This communication demands honesty, which invokes the moral component of integrity.

INTEGRITY: A FOUNDATION FOR INTEGRATION

The wholeness of an integrated project finds its expression in two ways. First, the project manager and the project team view a multiplexed project as a single system, with the interconnected parts all contributing to a successful outcome. Second, because of the need to communicate valid project data, information, and knowledge, the integration of the project builds on the personal integrity of all project personnel.

The words "integration" and "integrate" date from the 17th century. The word "integrity" predates them, having retained its meanings since the middle of the 16th century. [8] Integrity is an appropriate word for this subject because in its first sense it means whole, and the overarching spirit of this book is to consider all project parts holistically.

But the third and last sense of integrity comprises the moral sphere: "Soundness of moral principle; the character of uncorrupted virtue; uprightness, honesty, sincerity." Too many examples demonstrate forcefully the lack of these attributes in projects throughout the world.

Integrity is necessary for integration, and vice versa. As Napoleon explained in a famous line about battle plans—they work perfectly until contact with the enemy—the project as perfectly planned rarely exists in the execution phase. In fact, in contrast to the relatively contemplative iteration that can occur in the inception and development phases, one might replace the static-sounding terminology of the third major stage of a project, "implementation," with a name that better reflects that stage's activity: "real-time iteration."

In response to an alteration in one part of the project, the project team must iterate the entire plan if it wants to maintain the integrity of the project management system. More than at any other phase of the project, these iterations and integrations require the communication of valid, relevant data, information, and knowledge.

HONESTY AND PROFESSIONAL RESPONSIBILITY

Communication is the essence of project management, and communication implies honesty. If a measure of successful project management is the ability to trade off among the elements of the triple constraint, the project manager and the project team must depend on the transmission of good data and information to and from the project office.

But neither workers nor managers can claim to generate good project data if the data are not valid, i.e., if they do not answer the question asked, if they do not reflect reality. When they do, the project team can analyze these data from its already well-established integration perspective. Using the methods described in Chapter 4, changes in any one part of the schedule or budget, or of the overall scope, will be viewed in terms of all three elements. The process hinges on honesty, and the honesty begins with accepting and understanding the many details, some painful, of the project.

A profile of filmmaker Claude Lanzmann reported "in Lanzmann's moral register, detail is truth. Not the haze of memory, not the goodwill that is the exhaust of time's engine. Rigid, clear detail." [12] The same high standard should apply to project management, where details and honesty are two prime ingredients. If honesty has grades, then integration requires the highest: intellectual honesty. Intellectual honesty means that one attempts to understand, interpret, and communicate all relevant implications of the detailed data describing the project. In those details—data that one attempts to transform into information—lies the truth of the project's progress.

The integrative viewpoint reminds us always that one should not lose sight of the forest for the trees, but Lanzmann has demonstrated that a true understanding of the individual trees leads to a better view of the forest. Lanzmann's mission is to promulgate the idea "that one is responsible for what one does."

Integrative management progresses on responsibility. At a minimum, the responsibility includes dedication to the mechanics of the management itself, but in the truest sense of integration, it goes further. Projects fail for many reasons, but rarely, if ever, do they fail because of poor Gantt charts.

A project may fail because of a lack of resources, but if that were a good excuse, every project manager and team could use it! The job is to make things work. A project manager should understand the difference between power and authority, which is more than an academic nicety. In the hierarchical structure of the organization, upper management may limit a project manager's authority, but imagination and courage can expand the manager's personal power, i.e., the ability to accomplish ancillary tasks and remove obstacles.

Legitimate long-term use of personal power requires personal integrity; increasing personal integrity will increase potential personal power. A responsible project manager will use power for the good of the project and the project team. For example, in a matrix organizational structure, one may not possess the authority to reward team personnel directly with salary increases, but a good project manager will convey strong messages regarding a worker's good performance, not only to the worker but also to the worker's hierarchical superiors. Fulfillment of this responsibility to appreciate and recognize team personnel will improve team cohesiveness and performance, further team members' enthusiasm and concern for the project, and thus ultimately enhance the proper integration of the project's management.

The article about Lanzmann also characterized his attitudes about responsibility as "unpopular" and "uncomfortable" today, when what is most valued is "redemption." [12] One representation of the *zeitgeist* is reflected by the common saying, "it is easier to ask for forgiveness than permission": Allow projects to overrun their budgets and ignore their schedules, and in the end not meet specifications anyway—then ask for more funds and more time, excusing management failures. An honest, authentic management culture abhors such behavior.

SHARING INFORMATION MEANS SHARING POWER

Project personnel should communicate data honestly and thus share power (which was the subversive agenda of Chapter 2). In the context of project management information systems, for example, Graham and Englund write of sharing data to relieve anxiety. [14] Anyone who has waited at an airport, speculating about possible reasons for a plane's delay, knows that a lack of information generates anxiety. As discussed, Leibniz saw integration as a means of acquiring and organizing knowledge, and he may have appreciated this notion of data as anxiety relief. How do data fulfill this function?

Data establish a foundation for planning and for subsequent actions that favor the best project results. Sharing data gives project personnel potential power. That is, freed from a stifling dependency upon hierarchical superiors, project personnel should retain the ability to accomplish tasks that move the project forward; they also retain the responsibility.

Senior executives and the project manager are responsible for establishing the conditions that encourage honest communication and shared power. Does this concept of responsibility fit with the modern view of management? It depends on whom you ask. Go outside the management establishment and consider the opinion of the open-source culture. In the jargon dictionary one finds: "management n. 1. Corporate power elites distinguished primarily by their distance from actual productive work and their chronic failure to manage (see also suit)." [27] With this definition, the strong words noted above—communication, freedom, integrity, honesty, and perhaps most of all, responsibility—do not come to the fore.

On the other hand, consider what management guru Peter Drucker wrote nearly 30 years ago in *Tasks, Responsibilities, Practices*: "Eiichi Shibusawa's Confucian ideal of the 'professional manager' has become reality. And so has Shibusawa's basic insight that the essence of the manager is neither wealth nor rank, but responsibility." [11]

The reality lies somewhere between the hope expressed by Drucker and the cynicism of the hackers, but if we judge from what is observed in projects around the world, the concept of responsible project management has not yet fully taken hold. Many projects that are portrayed as successful are often viewed deliberately through a distorting lens of a single, selected axis of the triple constraint or from plans rebaselined many times. Integrated projects are not possible without integrity.

INTEGRATION AND PROJECT SUCCESS

In any organization, integration begins with the right attitude by senior executives. This attitude manifests itself first with the choice of good projects, that is, projects consistent with the company's stated goals. The first integration is an integration of projects and vision.

The senior administration's respect (or lack thereof) for an integrated approach to managing projects will permeate the organization. Then, within any given project, integration begins with managing the information of the triple constraint: an internally consistent approach to the cost, schedule, and scope of the project.

Integration continues with building the project team and softening interfaces. The team then works to understand and, if possible, integrate the concerns of the wider parties at interest. This integration of people and people's ideas is at least as difficult and as important as integrating the project's numbers. Good, realistic planning with sufficient funding (which is redundant because integrated planning implies funding consistent with the scope and schedule) lays the foundation for a successful project, but success results from people's work.

This book began with a silly look at a typical lack of integration as portrayed in a futuristic movie. Do you remember, however, what happens later in *Return of the Jedi*? At the start of its attack on Death Star II, the rebel alliance discovers that the persuasive oratory of Darth Vader and the management skills of his cooperative project leader have had their effect: The seemingly incomplete sphere is a "fully armed and operational battle station."

So when surrounded by—and trying to integrate—resource breakdown structures, work breakdown structures, network diagrams, Gantt charts, effort distributions, and budgets, remember that projects are ultimately for and about people. Success, i.e., meeting the triple constraint, depends ultimately on the cooperation of all the interested parties and on the hard work of project personnel. Integrating the numbers and the people is the height of professional project management. Leibniz would be pleased.

Bibliography and Notes

1. Amabile, Teresa M. "How to Kill Creativity." *Harvard Business Review*, September–October 1998, p. 78.
2. Anbari, Frank. *An Operating Management Control System for Large Scale Projects.* American Institute for Decision Sciences, Ninth Annual Meeting, Northeast Regional Conference (Philadelphia, 1980).
3. Augustine, Charles, and Daniel Dreyer. "Inception." Chapter in *Project Management Handbook.* George Washington University students in Management 268 (Summer Session), *Project Management Applications* (Washington, D.C., June 2000).
4. Bailetti, A.J., J.R. Callahan, and P. DiPietro. "A Coordination Structure Approach to the Management of Projects." *IEEE Transactions on Engineering Management* (November 1994).
5. Benningson, L.A. "TREND: A Project Management Tool." *Proceedings of the Project Management Conference* (Philadelphia, October 1972).
6. Berlinski, David. *A Tour of the Calculus* (New York: Pantheon Books, 1995).
7. Brooks, Frederick P., Jr. *The Mythical Man-Month,* 20th anniversary edition (Boston: Addison Wesley, 1995).
8. Brown, Lesley. Ed. *The New Shorter Oxford English Dictionary* (Clarendon Press, 1993).
9. The Calculus Period. Britannica CD. Version 2001. (Encyclopedia Britannica, Inc., 2000).
10. Cioffi, Denis. "Learning from Hackers." *IEEE Spectrum*, 38(6), June 2001.
11. Drucker, Peter. *Management: Tasks, Responsibilities, Practices* (New York: Harper and Row, 1973).
12. Fisher, Marc. "The Truth That Can Only Hurt." *The Washington Post* (June 25, 1999).
13. Frame, David. *The New Project Management* (San Francisco: Jossey-Bass, 1994).
14. Graham, Robert J., and Randall L. Englund. *Creating an Environment for Successful Projects* (San Francisco: Jossey-Bass Publishers, 1997), p. 136.
15. Harr, Jonathan. *A Civil Action* (New York: Vintage Books, 1995). The test is described in "Billion-Dollar Charlie," section 7.
16. Jaques, Elliott. *Requisite Organization: A Total System for Effective Managerial Organization and Managerial Leadership for the 21st Century,* 2nd revised edition (Arlington, VA: Cason Hall & Co, 1998).
17. Kerzner, Harold. *Project Management: A Systems Approach to Planning, Scheduling, and Controlling,* 7th edition (New York: John Wiley and Sons, Inc., 1998).
18. Kerzner, Harold. *Applied Project Management: Best Practices on Implementation* (New York: John Wiley and Sons, Inc., 2000).
19. Lawrence, Paul R., and Jay W. Lorsch. "New Management Job: The Integrator." *Harvard Business Review*, 45(6), November–December 1967.

20. Levy, Paul F. "The Nut Island Effect: When Good Teams Go Wrong." *Harvard Business Review*, March 2001, pp. 52–59.

21. Meredith, J. R., and S. J. Mantel. *Project Management: A Managerial Approach,* 4th ed. (New York: John Wiley and Sons, Inc., 2000).

22. Merrifield, D. Bruce. "Changing Nature of Competitive Advantage." *Research Technology Management*, January–February 2000, pp. 41–45. Part of a special series, *Succeeding in Technological Innovation.*

23. Naff, Kevin C. "A look at...mydotcom@work." *The Washington Post*, March 11, 2001, p. B3.

24. Project Management Institute. *Project Management Professional (PMP) Role Delineation Study* (Newton Square, PA: Project Management Institute, Inc., 2000).

25. Project Management Institute Standards Committee. *A Guide to the Project Management Body of Knowledge (PMBOK® Guide).* (Newton Square, PA: Project Management Institute, 2000).

26. Rad, Parviz F. *Project Estimating and Cost Management.* (Vienna, VA: Management Concepts, Inc., 2002), Chapter 3, coauthored with Denis F. Cioffi.

27. Raymond, Eric S. Jargon File Resources. www.tuxedo.org /~esr/jargon/, January 31, 2000. Version 4.2.0.

28. Tan, G.W., C.C. Hayes, and M. Shaw. "An Intelligent-Agent Framework for Concurrent Product Design and Planning." *IEEE Transactions on Engineering Management*, August 1996.

29. Tufte, Edward R. *The Visual Display of Quantitative Information*, 2nd ed. (Cheshire, CT: Graphics Press, 1983).

30. Tufte, Edward R. *Envisioning Information* (Cheshire, CT: Graphics Press, 1990).

31. Tufte, Edward R. *Visual Explanations* (Cheshire, CT: Graphics Press, 1997).

32. Tufte, Edward R. Lecture: "Presenting Data and Information," Crystal City, VA, May 8, 2001. (A slightly different listing of these principles can be found in *Visual Explanations.*)

33. Verzuh, Eric. *The Fast Forward MBA in Project Management* (New York: John Wiley and Sons, Inc., New York, 1999).

34. Wells, Jim. National Ignition Facility. http://www.gao.gov/new.items/rc00141.pdf, Aug.2000.

35. Wilson, Edward O. *Consilience* (New York: Alfred E. Knopf, 1998), p. 147.

Index